I Am My
Mother's Daughter

I Am My
Mother's Daughter

Making Peace with Mom—
Before It's Too Late

Iris Krasnow

BASIC
BOOKS

A Member of the Perseus Books Group
New York

Copyright © 2006 by Iris Krasnow
Hardcover published in 2006 by Basic Books
A Member of the Perseus Books Group
Paperback published in 2007 by Basic Books

Designed by Jeff Williams
Set in Fairfield Light by the Perseus Books Group

Library of Congress Cataloging-in-Publication Data
    Krasnow, Iris.
    I am my mother's daughter : making peace with mom before it's too late / Iris Krasnow.
        p. cm.
    Includes bibliographical references.
    HC: ISBN-13: 978-0-465-03754-4; ISBN-10: 0-465-03754-2
    1. Mothers. 2. Daughters. 3. Mothers and daughters. 4. Inter-personal conflict.   I. Title.
    HQ759.K724 2005
    306.874'3—dc22

                                                        2005035494

PBK: ISBN-13: 978-0-465-03755-1; ISBN-10: 0-465-03755-0

10 9 8 7 6 5 4 3

For my mother
Helene Steinberg Krasnow

Contents ✤

Prologue 🌿

It's a balmy afternoon in late May, and I am pushing my mother in her wheelchair along the lakefront in Chicago, the city where I was born fifty years ago and where she soon will die. With unwavering courage, defying all odds, my mom, Helene, survived the loss of her immediate family to the Holocaust, the loss of her husband in 1986, and the recent loss of her lower left leg. After this heroic marathon, she's now barely hanging on, plagued with infections, dementia, and total exhaustion.

Yet, we are fully present in this moment and not dwelling on her demise; the sun is brilliant and the breezes off Lake Michigan are gently slapping us into sheer wakefulness. I look down at my mother with the paisley pashmina draped over her stump; she used to wear it as a shawl. Her cheeks are flushed and she is smiling. May is the month when spring is most saturated, the trees are thick, the flowers are lush. We stop at a patch of tulips near Oak Street Beach, a triumph of purple and yellow, pink and red. Their petals are widely spread, about to scatter on the ground.

"The tulips are going, Iya. But your mother is alive," she whispers, reaching feebly for a flower. Iya is my childhood nickname, and lately every time she calls me that the confluence of love and imminent loss is almost too much to bear. I know she is thinking what I am thinking—of the tulip beds we had in our backyard in the house where she raised three children, in nearby Oak Park. We are thinking how the span of our lives goes as swiftly as a blast of wind off the lake. We are thinking that flower petals scatter with the seasons and that children scatter across the country. My sister, Frances, stayed in the Chicago area, but my brother, Greg, lives in California, and I settled in Maryland.

I am my mother's daughter, so I know what she is thinking—because we share a heart.

I reach for her hand, gnarled with arthritis, and make small talk about the mussels we are about to eat at her favorite French bistro and the sterling silver jewelry sale we are about to hit at Lord & Taylor. For twenty-seven years she stood on two feet as a saleswoman at that store on Michigan Avenue. Today she is wheeled in, and when other customers gawk at the old woman with one leg sitting regally in her chair, I am sharply reminded of why I wrote this book on mothers and adult daughters and rage and resolution.

I love my mother unfailingly now. Yet, during a defiant adolescence and my early adult years, I sometimes felt that I hated her. My love for her, so deep this minute it frightens me, was discovered almost too late—as she lay in a near coma two years ago, after the amputation. She fooled her doctors and her three children and eight grandchildren; she didn't die as everyone expected. So I got some bonus time to make peace with my charming, formidable, difficult mother who has turned into my friend, my drinking partner, my primary link to myself and my destiny.

Grateful for, and astonished by, the journey that brought my mother and me to this place, I was curious to discover how other midlife daughters are navigating this tough but crucial passage. Are they, too, moving from malaise to reconciliation? Are they able to push through old anger and increasingly draw sustenance from the primal, omnipotent maternal bond? I also wanted to see how other baby-boomer daughters compared the mothers they have now to the mothers they battled at fifteen.

I didn't have to look far for people to interview. At the mere mention of the title, heads would nod, sighs would heave, eyes would roll. I'd start out with, "So tell me about your mother," and daughters eagerly spilled everything, from memories of cloying adoration to incidents of unimaginable violence. It seems that every graying woman has something compelling to share about aging along with her mother, power grannies who are living longer than ever.

Over the past year, I've collected more than a hundred stories, like precious beads, some as dark as black pearls, others like luminous sapphires, and strung them into an expansive female soul circle. Our conversations lasted from several hours to several days, taking place over cups of coffee or glasses of wine in kitchens across the country, from San Francisco to Dallas to the Adirondack region of New York. The women who generously allowed me to excavate their histories are rich, poor, black, white, gay, and straight and span ages thirty-four to seventy. Although some of the daughters I interviewed have lost their moms, this is not a book about dealing with death; it's about dealing with mothers in this lifetime.

The stories on these pages are raw, startling, and most important, true. They resonate with prescriptions on how to kiss and make up and move on. Although the women's backgrounds vary, their experiences have brought them to this common conclusion: Ditching old baggage and learning to love our mothers must come before we learn to love, and know, ourselves. And the pain that comes from losing a mother you're still fighting with is a suffering that doesn't subside. Some of the women requested that their real names be used. Those who wished to remain anonymous picked their own pseudonyms, and identifying details were changed. Here are some of the women you will meet.

Janine grew up on a farm in Georgia with a mother who beat her with a horsewhip. Ellen became a binge eater to fill up on the love she never got at home. As Adrienne's mother lay dying, she flipped her estranged daughter the finger. Chynna speaks of feeling emotionally abandoned by her rock-star mother, Michelle Phillips, one of the mamas in The Mamas and the Papas. Rebecca's mother hollered so much during her childhood that this daughter is raising her own kids in a home where raising your voice is forbidden. Grace's mom carted around a heavy toolbox and could build virtually anything, from couches to carports. Grace is now dealing with the agonizing transition that many adult daughters are going through—the morphing of a supermom into a sad, needy widow. Erica came out as a lesbian around the same time her mother outed her own secret, that she was engaged in a long-term affair.

Despite their diverse histories, all of these daughters have embraced their mothers. And if they can't forgive them for unforgivable acts, at least they are willing to forget the past and move forward. This takes enough maturity to understand that the meanest of mothers is often the product of her own lack of mothering or her own stormy past. Along with horror stories, this book also contains lots of love stories, such as the one about Juanita, a daughter in her sixties who never left her mother's house, becoming her nurse until she died of Alzheimer's. Then there's Rita, a brilliant executive who spent many years frustrated that her mother, a voluptuous blond widow, goes to bars at night instead of tackling intellectual pursuits. At the age of fifty, Rita stopped obsessing about their differences and now joins her mom at the neighborhood pub. During these Cabernet-laced sessions of honest girl-talk, Rita has discovered what many grown daughters I interviewed are finding out about their mothers: "The mirrors are everywhere." The book also contains sagas filled with more subtle annoyances that routinely come up between mothers and daughters, scuffles that reflect the line I heard time and time again: "My mother is a pain, but I love her anyway."

Thanks to medical advances and the rise in senior fitness, we, their daughters, have an elongated second chance to smooth out the connection and to get it right. Women in their nineties are the fastest-growing segment of the aging population. That means a daughter of fifty may be sitting at the holiday table with her mother for the next twenty years, marking a new, previously undocumented passage in the female life cycle. Your own mother may be a tennis champ with a younger boyfriend and not on her last leg, like mine.

But that doesn't mean you can be lazy and put off working on the relationship. I know this firsthand, because I was late in the game to patch things up, and I am now racing to love my mom as much I can, while I still have her within reach. The best time to start the process of pushing through antique pain and vintage blame is when your mother is healthy, and not when you're on deathwatch, like me. Your reward will be precious bonus years of a supportive friendship with the woman who has known you longer and better, and loves you more, than any other person on earth.

On these pages, menopausal daughters talk about giggling with mothers they used to despise, swapping stories about arthritis and eyelifts and dating. Even those with the most horrific pasts have chosen to suck it up and accept their imperfect mothers, lowering their expectations and opening their hearts. Those women who come to healthy completion in their relationships speak about how a mother's death can even be emancipating. When a mother passes on, a midlife woman is freed to take the best of her, leave the worst behind, and become wholly her own person. The journey can be lonely, but it is also a rich adventure, as grieving daughters turn to spiritual exploration, tackling new dreams and deepening their friendships with other women. I know that my girlfriends, my personal soul circle, will be there to help me heal. They already have.

I am just back from three days in Santa Fe where four women I've known for thirty years gathered for a reunion at a mountain retreat. We are all fifty and our mothers are still alive. We laugh and cry about everything: old boyfriends, current husbands, good mothers, bad mothers, and how we will cope when we are orphans. It's a Saturday morning, and we are lying naked on a cedar deck, wet from the hot tub. The air is cool, but we are warmed by the blazing sun and snug in the womb of the cliffs that encase us. At this instant, I have a clear vision of four fifty-year-old women being reborn.

We have emerged from the water, and we are wet, like infants newly plucked from the amniotic sac. Only this rebirth in New Mexico is not as daughters but as wise women accountable only to ourselves. Like babies, we will always crave comfort and love, but we can get that by staying connected to our long-standing circle of goddess girlfriend energy. As I continue to age and lose other loved ones, I will always find solace with the cluster of sisters I met in my youth, who still anchor me with light and love. Our mothers may move out of this world, but their spirits will be part of that circle, as will the spirits of grandmothers, great-grandmothers, and Mother Earth.

Listening to the rousing voices of the women who animate these chapters reinforces the urgency of working hard to form a mother-daughter bond built on compassion and surrender. By learning to love our mothers, we are free to become our strongest, truest selves. May this book propel you on your own urgent journey to find peace with your mother and peace with yourself.

chapter one

I Love You,
I Hate You, I Am You

*To become optimally healthy and happy, each of us
must get clear about the ways in which our
mother's history both influenced and continues to
inform our state of health, our beliefs, and how we
live our lives.*

—Christiane Northrup, M.D.

I CAN'T SHAKE A RECENT CONVERSATION with a forty-
four-year-old neighbor who is seeing her mother at Thanksgiving for the first time in eight years. This reunion also marks
the first time an eighty-one-year-old grandma meets her two

grandchildren, ages six and eight. I told my girlfriend to kiss and make up over a glass of wine, that it may be the last time she ever sees her mom, and you can't say "let's work this out" at a funeral.

My father's shocking death at the age of sixty-seven and my mother's increasing frailty after the recent amputation of her leg have taught me the importance of meeting our parents with surrender and softened hearts while we have them within reach, and not when all we are left with are faded photographs and regrets.

The final meal I had with my dad was Thanksgiving, nineteen years ago, in our family home in downtown Chicago. Our relationship was solid; there was no rift. Yet, if I had known this was our last supper, I would have said "thank you" a thousand times for his unrelenting support, as I wedged my face into the crook of his neck, my comfort spot as a child. I tell him lots of things now that I never got to tell him, and I hope he is listening and still feels his daughter's love. I will not make the same mistake with my mother, whom I never loved as much as I did my dad—until he was gone and she was the only parent left. He used to protect me from her sharply shifting moods; now I must face her naked, honest, and alone.

In my last book, *Surrendering to Yourself*, I looked hard at the need to live urgently, as if this day were our last, through the eyes of people who suffer from terminal illnesses or who have endured the sudden loss of loved ones. Keenly aware of the eggshell-thin line that separates the splendor of life from the ravages of death, they speak of taking swift action now to fix relationships that are broken. I am taking swift action to discover the lingering mysteries surrounding my mom, now a wisp of her former self and in and out of dementia.

The Thanksgiving confluence of emotions and tradition seems to trigger epiphanies about my parents. Two Thanksgivings ago, my eighty-three-year-old mother, who at the time had both legs, is visiting my Annapolis home from Chicago. She is sitting at the head of our mahogany kitchen table, surrounded by four grandsons, then thirteen, eleven, and nine-year-old twins. I am kneading clumps of hot sweet potatoes and drizzling the mixture with butter, as I listen to my mother tell the boys to finish every speck of food on their plates, to sit up straight, to say thank you when food is passed. Hearing her nag and poke resurrects piercing childhood memories, and I feel my stomach lurch the same way it lurched when she harped at me as a girl. Something stops me from biting back, and in that moment—suspended between getting mad or letting it slide—I am deeply thankful on Thanksgiving. At least I still have a mother.

My husband, Chuck, is an orphan, and despite our bounty of noisy kids, every holiday, indeed part of every day, will forever be somewhat hollow for him. So more and more, I let my mother "be," as the Buddhists tell us to do; I flow with the currents of the river instead of flailing against them. She will not change. The only change I have the power to control, I am realizing, is how I react to her. So I am learning not to attack when she says someone is fat or ugly or should be wearing lipstick—always when that person is within earshot. I do not snap back when she tells me my hair is too gray or that my clothes look cheap. Knowing that soon, too soon, she won't be here to complain about, I grasp tightly to the moments when I am with her. Indeed, I have come to love her in ways I never before loved her, as I've unraveled new layers of her character that are mischievous and whimsical.

On my last visit to Chicago, my mom told me that as a teenager in Warsaw she used to ride on the back seat of motorcycles driven by boys, her long, curly hair flying. They would "get lost" in the Polish countryside. "My mother couldn't control me," she said with a little wink and a wry smile. I love that image of her, in defiant abandon, and it leaves me wondering, What else did she do? What else should I know? The intrigue is seductive and makes me hungry to root around in her past, but sadly these girl-talk sessions are dwindling as her banter is increasingly random and indecipherable. Having finally achieved an easy and fun friendship after years of strife, and some staggering wars, I already feel the lonely sting of loss that lies ahead.

Yet even after the nastiest of exchanges, we kissed and made up and moved on. The fists-up hostility I used to feel is all but gone. But there are still times when the old, bad blood surfaces. This ironically occurs when I'm enjoying my sons, hands in dirt, planting seeds, or hands in clay, getting filthy, laughing. In these transcendent moments I am reminded of how few sentimental vignettes involving my mother I can conjure up. Helene Krasnow did not play with me. Nor did she mentor me in her domesticity or style, of which there was an abundance.

She wore beautiful gold jewelry but never spread out her treasures on the bed and told me about each one of them, as my girlfriends' moms did with them. My mother's jewelry chest was hidden under piles of underwear in her top drawer, her sign to "keep out." She wore Shalimar, a spicy and intoxicating fragrance I adored, but she refused to spray any on me—"It's expensive," she would say. I am a good cook, but not because of her culinary skills. No child was allowed in her kitchen when she was preparing meals. I first turned on an oven in my fifth-grade home economics class.

While my mother made supper, my sister, Frances, and I would each practice thirty minutes of piano to the cold tick of the metronome. This was a surefire way to keep us out of my mother's warm kitchen, and believe me, it was *her* kitchen. And so my signature dishes, from Caesar salad to garlic roasted chicken, I copied from recipes of other mothers who let me huddle next to them at their stoves. I have no daughters to display my jewelry for or to dab with my favorite rose oil scent. But I encourage my sons to stand shoulder to shoulder with me in *our* kitchen and learn my secrets for potato pancakes or a meat loaf of ground beef and black beans. When I'm gone, my recipes will live on, and my boys will be fathers making meat loaf with their children, remembering how Grandma Iris was crazy about cooking, and how she turned their kitchen into a sacred, shared space.

To this day, when I smell roasting garlic or Shalimar, I have to catch my breath as some of the hurt of my girlhood wafts through me. Mashing the sweet potatoes during my mother's Thanksgiving visit, I am tempted to snarl about how different we are—I being the generous and open mother, and she the closed, selfish one.

"Remember how *you* used to mash potatoes and I couldn't come near you," I nearly blurt out. But thankfully, I hold my tongue. I am melting at the sight of an old, failing lady sitting at the table with four hardy grandsons. They are rapt, mouths open, hypnotized by the sheer force of Grandma, her Slavic accent, and stories of resilience and survival. Every chance she gets, she tells them how lucky they are to be fed, clothed, and free—luxuries they take for granted and that she had to fight for when she was young.

During the German occupation of Europe, seventeen-year-old Helene fled her hometown of Warsaw for Paris. Her parents and older siblings with children of their own stayed behind, too settled in their professions to move and not believing the buzz among Jews that the Nazis were determined to exterminate every one of them. My mother was taken in by a Catholic woman named Pupette, who encouraged her to burn the papers that said "Helene Steinberg" and become the non-Jewish "Helene Moreaux." The pseudonym allowed my mom to live openly with Pupette in Paris for the next twelve years, going to church every Sunday and working as an usher in a movie house. Each day, when she escorted the Nazi soldiers to their seats, her heart would thump in fear that one of them had come on a tip that the curly-haired usher with the deep dimples was actually Jewish. My mother often tells stories of fooling the Nazis at the movies, always ending it this way: "I should have brought a knife in my pocket and stabbed them all."

While she lived safely in Paris, her mother, brother, sister, and seven nieces and nephews were rounded up and murdered in Hitler's death camps. (Her father died of heart failure before their deportation.) As a young child, I didn't understand why my mom was so callous, because she only revealed her horrific history slowly, over many years. As an adult, I see that her early and unspeakable loss encased her in an often-impenetrable shell. She knew too well the danger of loving too much: People you love could be gone in a finger snap. When my father died in 1986, rather than succumb to a black gloom, my freshly widowed sixty-five-year-old mother dressed up in blazers and silk scarves and sold men's clothing at the Lord & Taylor on Chicago's Michigan Avenue, a job she held until she was eighty. She says of her ability to spring back, again and again: "If the Nazis didn't get me, nothing can." I may not have always appreciated the direction she was going in, but one thing is certain: Her ability to keep moving forward, pushing through enormous pain, is astounding.

Reflecting on the shades and twists and texture of her life, I picture an Indian-print tapestry, swirled with somber colors, rippled with knots where it has been sewn, some swatches worn so thin they are about to tear. My mother has lasted so long; she is winding down and will be leaving soon. This I know, so I am much better behaved than I used to be, as on this day in my kitchen when my entire past fuses into one intense flash of awareness that the tomorrows with her are few. I am more grateful about who she is than incensed by who she is not. More and more, I allow her to have the final word during any heated conversation, whereas in the past, getting in the last stab meant everything to me.

I am relieved that we didn't spar over that Thanksgiving weekend when she was digging into my kids, because three months later, my self-absorbed and indestructible mother would be lying in Chicago's Northwestern Hospital, her lower left leg amputated, close to death from the shock of the procedure. I slept at the hospital the night of her surgery and was standing by her bed the morning she woke up, missing one foot and half a calf. She looked at the empty space on the sheet where her full left leg should have been and then looked at her daughter. This was a stare of such burning despair that it shot through my body like shrapnel. A mother reassures her child, "Don't worry, honey, it's going to be all right." In that instant, I wanted to mother my own mother and assure her, "You're going to be just fine." But no words came out because I knew she wasn't going to be just fine again, nor would I. My invincible mother was now little more than a broken doll, who could not move unless she was moved, who could not eat unless she was fed, and who could not walk because she had one foot. Although dulled by the anesthesia, she was sharply aware that horror had struck her once again.

"What did they do? Why did you let them? Oh my God," she said, reaching with a shaking hand for her shortened leg. When she fell back asleep I forced myself to pull up the white cotton blanket to see the cast that ended four inches below the knee. Exhaling sharply, my heart exploding, I put my forehead on her thigh and cried, wishing like a child that her leg would grow back. "Mom, I love you, I love you," I said over and over. She looked down at me with dead brown eyes and whispered, "I know you do."

My brother, Greg, says it is a gift from our mom to her three children that she is dying one piece at a time and not all at once. It gives us a jump start on the process of grieving and acceptance while she is still around. Knowing that the end is near slaps us into urgent action to work out any remaining rage we have festering between us. I know that the only way I can be a woman, a lover, and a nurturing mother who is grounded and whole is to resolve and complete my relationship with Helene Krasnow, whom I love now and often detested in the past.

Seven months after her surgery, the weekend before Thanksgiving 2004, my tipsy mother is being twirled in a black wheelchair in the center of a dance floor at the Annapolis Marriott on the Chesapeake Bay. Some two hundred guests at my son Isaac's Bar Mitzvah are doing a frenzied horah around her, clapping and sweating, laughing and crying. My mother's mouth is wide open, her arms are outstretched in a triumphant V, and her remaining leg is kicking wildly. In one hand, she is swinging the maroon cloth dinner napkin, her pinky is arched—always the lady, regal. Not much has changed over the decades she has been my mother. She is still Her Majesty Helene, and Her Highness still reigns.

"I ain't dead yet," she tells me when the last stanza of "Hava Nagila" sounds; she is clutching a martini, her fingernails glistening in the opal lacquer she has always worn. She did it—she confounded the doctors and her kids and didn't die as she nearly did a dozen times over the past months, from loss of blood, infections, fevers. She lived to upstage her grandson at his Bar Mitzvah.

"What Lola wants Lola gets," she says, winking and grinning. "I told myself 'Helene, you will live until your grandson's Bar Mitzvah,' and here I am. I resisted death." Here she is, indeed—in bright red lipstick, a black Chico's pantsuit, with a red and turquoise silk scarf twirling around her neck. A month earlier, she was lying in a near coma in a Chicago hospital with a temperature of 103.

Tonight she's at a party, and I bend down to her wheelchair, inhaling the scent of Shalimar, and whisper in her ear: "Don't die yet, Mom. You gotta dance at the twins' Bar Mitzvah two years from now." I think of her unwavering courage, of not caving in to depression after losing parents, siblings, husband,

and now a limb. I still smell her perfume as I walk away to get my own martini, teary and wondering, "Who will I be when she is no longer here?" I love her now more than ever.

Yet, I've often felt that I hated my mother. A couple of years ago, irked to the edge, I even did the unthinkable: I said "F—k you" to her, right in my driveway, on a sunny Saturday in April, just before 3 P.M. We had taken my sons shopping at the Annapolis Mall, and when we returned home, instead of patiently waiting for Grandma—who was agile then—and helping her from her seat, they slammed the car doors, bolted in four directions, and ignored her.

"Your sons have no manners. They're brats," she hissed, and made a face like she was sucking on a lemon (in Yiddish this look is described as a *Ferbisinapunim*). Well, my kids are a lot of things, including sloppy and loud. But they are not brats, and they are not ill mannered. In fact, their behavior is downright worshipful toward their grandmother, who holds court at my kitchen table, as the kids fetch olives for her martini and serenade her on the piano with Beethoven's "Für Elise." Her attack brought up a geyser of hurtful memories. I am ten again, and she is calling me a "brat full of venom." So I shot out the F-word, decades after the first time I wanted to say it.

I will never forget the look she shot back. Her face turned gray, her mouth quivered. Then words burbled forth like hot lava. "I know that you hate me. You have always hated me. I am leaving," she said, walking quickly into the house and into the guest room where she flung her black suitcase onto the bed, its roller-wheels sticking out from the mattress's edge like a dead animal's feet.

I stared at the wheels. Wheels mean movement, that someone is going away, and maybe this pissed-off mother of mine is going away for good. Maybe her plane will crash, or disintegrate at 32,000 feet. Then I will writhe forever in agony about our last time together when I said the worst thing you can say to your mother. And she will look down at me from her throne in heaven feeling smug and satisfied that she got me last.

She flew home to Chicago a day early and did not die, and our relationship didn't wither either. In fact, out of the ashes of that fire a better relationship was born. In the phone conversations that came after our explosion, I said I was sorry over and over, sorry for the words, but not sorry that I had erupted. Because it gave me a chance to exhume my truth. And from this explosion came the death of the fantasy mom and the birth of what is real—a necessary step to moving a relationship along. When the F-word went flying, all artificial niceties between us were dissolved, for good.

I got to tell my mom that she had been too harsh on me as a girl and that there was no genetic license allowing her to rip into my sons. "They are mine to reprimand, not yours," I told her, and then told her more. That she was unmotherly, had never baked cookies with me, had never lain on my bed and read to me, had never taken me to fancy stores for girly things, that the only school clothes she bought were ordered from Sears catalogs. I told her that Terry Schwartz's mother used to fold love poems into her bag lunches and that all I got was bologna and cheese.

I told her I felt my father was my mother while I was growing up. He was the one who took me to the zoo, drove me to art lessons, sat patiently outside the dressing room at Marshall Field's while I tried on white button-down blouses and Villager wool kilts. He was the one who put his arm around me while we watched Walter Cronkite deliver the evening news, stroking stray wisps of hair off my forehead. He was the one I ran to in the middle of the night when a bad dream shook me awake. I would sit on the top of the stairs, and he would go downstairs in his navy-plaid bathrobe, warm a pot of milk on the stove, spoon honey into it, and then lie next to me in my bed while I sipped this calming brew and was lulled back to sleep. I dreaded the days he was out of town on business trips because I knew if a nightmare hit at 2 A.M. I was on my own.

I did not dare to wake my mother for something as piddly as a bad dream, because if I did, she would order me back to bed, reminding me that I was a big girl who could take care of myself. When I was six and sobbing on the porch because our family friend Ruth had died, the first time someone I actually knew had died, she scolded me for grieving.

"Stop crying. Everyone dies," snapped this witness to the Nazi purge of an entire civilization.

Throughout our talks, she listened stoically as I went on. Her ultimate response to my long list of gripes was brief: "You didn't turn out so bad. There was always food on the table, and I did the best I could." Those words were as bracing as an icy shower. I'm struck by the memories of visiting friends' homes when I was in elementary school. No adult would be in sight, and we were left to scrounge around the kitchen to piece together our own snacks or dinners. My mother may not have wanted company in her kitchen, but unfailingly, she was in there, like a machine, slicing, spreading, juggling hot pans. She fixed three complete meals a day for three children and set them at our places at the Formica dinette table, alongside glasses of milk, until we each left home at eighteen.

That she was doing the best that she could never occurred to me. Today I see that her regimentation and resolve formed my strongest qualities. Having a mother who didn't hover over me forced me to realize early on that I was indeed a big, strong girl who could take care of myself. Her stories of survival gave me the will to tackle life with purpose and perseverance. The slaughter of her family gave me the impetus to go out and replace the lives that were lost and to build a family on the foundation of Judaism. Four children that resulted from this fervor are blessings, my loves, my life.

My mother used to snap our window shades open at 6:45 A.M. as a wake-up call—no gentle nudges or morning kisses from this woman. Breakfast was at 7, lunch was at noon, dinner was at 5:30; bedtime was at 9:15. I shuddered at her drill sergeant precision. But decades later as I raise my own children on an identical schedule, I see that her obsession for routine gave my life structure and stability. You could count on my mother; she was always there. Yes, it is not so bad being her daughter. And we are probably more alike than I want to admit.

When we are sitting around my kitchen table, kids flying in and out, my mom often tells me that her happiest times were when my brother, sister, and I were all at home. "I had you all to myself," she says in a wistful whisper. "You kids were my life." I tell her that she sure had me fooled, because when I returned home from school she would be doing crossword puzzles and smoking Kents and sighing so deeply her shoulders would shake. She looked glum, not happy, wearing a red-checked dish towel over her shoulder, always ready to mop up the dirt we would track into the house. She was a fanatic about order and cleanliness; my girlhood home had plastic covers on the couches and chairs in the living room. In the summer, we had to strip off our sweaty clothes before entering the house.

My mother was smart and organized and could have run a company, or even a country. But she was trapped in that kitchen of the 1960s, along with most wives and mothers of that era. The highlight of the week was walking down the block to play Scrabble with her friend Shirley. To fill the time and to keep herself distracted from the pain of her own girlhood, she became an obsessive housekeeper—a "maniac housekeeper," as Simone de Beauvoir calls this brand of woman in *The Second Sex*.

I remember my mom whipping the dish towel off her shoulder to wipe up milk the second it spilled, or falling on her knees to pick up cold macaroni from under the kitchen table. Yet, in this last lap of life, she reflects on the mad feeding-cleaning frenzy of young motherhood four decades ago as a blissful state. And I can see why.

The Severn River glistens outside my window in the early sun, and I'm thinking of how much I love my own kitchen. The children are clamoring for cereal and bowls, and I sit with them at the same battered mahogany table where four babies sat in high chairs, as I spooned mashed peas into their tiny pink mouths. This Tuesday morning, my sons are devouring the fried eggs I just flipped out of a buttery pan, in a hurry before school. I am soaking in every nuance of every child, knowing that soon they will be college kids with stubble on their faces and girlfriends in their cars. And I will no longer control the kitchen that nourishes them. Just like my mother, I turned out to be a woman whose greatest joy comes from fluffing her nest.

My six-foot-three firstborn, a fifteen-year-old who doesn't let me kiss him anymore, gets up too quickly and knocks over his glass. As milk drips onto the floor, I flick the dish towel off my shoulder and get down on my hands and knees, all the while bitching at him about how clumsy he is. His black Converse shoes are near my face, and I shudder at their size—a size thirteen, my baby wears.

Chuck enters the kitchen, surveys the scene, and mutters to himself: "The apple doesn't fall too far from the tree. She's just like Grandma." Ha! I resented her as a child; she was always complaining, always cleaning. Now I am my mother, huffing about the mess in my kitchen, all the while wishing my kids would show up at my table for meals forever. I get angry over little things, like when they forget to put their napkins in their laps, because I love them so much I want them to be perfect. It hurts to love this much; I understand my mother's odd behavior much better now.

When do we become our mothers? The transformation creeps up on us silently—or was it always there?

It's January 1, 2005, and I'm in Chicago celebrating New Year's Day with my mom in her apartment. She is pasty and bony but alive. Her wheelchair is pulled close to the kitchen table, which is still her favorite place to sit. We are eating bulging mussels left over from our dinner the previous evening at a French bistro. With a shaky but determined hand, she clutches half a shell, scoops up garlicky wine broth from the bottom of the bowl and slurps it down noisily. She is wearing a black terry-cloth sweat suit, and I open my eyes and my heart to drink in everything she is—her hunched shoulders, the pant leg hanging over her stump, the girlish glimmer, be it ever so slight, in her cloudy brown eyes.

She offers me a hand of bent fingers that is wet with mussel juice and tells me the damp weather is making her joints hurt badly. I reach for my purse and retrieve the shea butter cream I rub into my own hands when my arthritis acts up. As I massage her left hand, she closes her eyes, throws her head back, and smiles. I am wishing that I could repair her gnarled hands, but all I can do is keep repairing our relationship.

My plane departs in two and a half hours, and I must leave for Midway airport early to hustle through the Sunday traffic after the holiday weekend. I hug the breath out of her, pressing my cheek against her cheek, which feels like cold velvet. "I love you, Mom," I tell her, putting on my pea coat and circling my neck with a wool scarf. She reminds me to put on gloves. When I was ten and she told me to put on my gloves, I fussed that it wasn't cold enough. She would stand by the door until I put them on, but I'd yank them off as soon as I cleared the backyard.

At fifty, I put on my gloves and leave them on and am thrilled I still have a mother who worries about whether my hands are warm.

"I love you too, Iya," she answers, using the nickname of my youth. As I reach for the doorknob, I turn around and stare at her again. She looks up from her wheelchair and our eyes lock through a narrow tunnel of light. I am not seeing an old woman. I am seeing my mother at her fiftieth birthday party in a silver-sequined dress, sprawled on the piano, singing French love songs.

"I want you to be happy. I was happy," she adds.

For my mother to tell me that she was happy is the best gift she can give her daughter. This releases me, I am free. I don't have to stew in guilt that I could have done more, been more, that I could have somehow fixed her life. I see now that her life was not broken, and the only life I am capable of making or breaking is my own.

"I was happy," my mom is telling me. This from a woman whose closest family was burned in Nazi ovens when she was in her teens. At sixty-five, she watched her husband die during a California vacation from sloppy care in a small hospital where he was taken after his heart attack. Instead of re-treating, she put on pretty clothes and a smile and went out to sell menswear, saving her tears for the nighttime when she ate dinner alone. At eighty-five, she is trying to learn to walk again on a fake leg that looks good but feels awful on her raw stump.

Yet, overall, she considers her life to be happy and I know this now and will never forget it when she is gone. It's the greatest lesson a parent can pass on to a child: "Life will deal you inevitable blows, but you must not be destroyed by ex-ternal circumstances. Be strong within. You are in control of your own happiness."

"Don't die yet, Mom," I'm thinking in the Checker Cab en route to Midway airport. I need time to find out exactly how you bolted out of bed each morning and didn't surrender to misery. I need to hear how to be brave, too, when I'm facing my own goblins. I need this formula to pass on to my own children. Does a daughter ever stop needing something more from her mother?

The next day, I buy a tiny bottle of Shalimar perfume. It is very expensive, $116. No wonder she never let me use hers.

chapter two

LETTING GO OF
THE FANTASY MOM

The truth shall set you free.

—JOHN 8:32

SATISFIED WIVES WHO SHARE the formula for marital longevity in my book *Surrendering to Marriage* have much to teach midlife daughters clucking over the foibles of their mothers: Lowering expectations can lead to long-term happiness. Expecting perfection in an intense familial relationship is an unattainable fantasy that brings constant disappointment. Real mothers, like real partners, snore too much, spend too much, drink too much, yell too much, watch too much TV. Of course, these same folks can still dazzle with their sunny sides. But the dream mate or mythical mama who is a geyser of loving-kindness exists only in films and in your imagination—and in rare homes like Annette's, whose story comes later in this chapter.

As you grate against each other year after year, a fantasy mom, like a fantasy lover, is ground down to just another flawed human who can be very good or very bad—sometimes within the span of twenty minutes. Lowering expectations doesn't mean settling for dregs. It means you stop pitying yourself and consider yourself lucky if you're getting these essentials: a mother who is respectful, fights for you, shows up when she says she's going to show up, and periodically says "I love you." This is more than what many daughters have. So wipe away the fairy dust and embrace what is, and you just might find Mick Jagger is right on in his raspy anthem that holds this promise: "You can't always get what you want, but you get what you need."

In this chapter, Grace explains how she is getting exactly what she needs—the power from her internal reserves to accept that her illusory "Superwoman" mother is now whiny and weak, incapable of being her daughter's pillar any longer. Erica recounts how she and her late mother both shook loose from their fantasy perceptions of each other at the same time. When Erica came out to her mother as a lesbian, her mother came clean to Erica about her longtime affair with "the love of her life," a man she eventually married. By realizing that her mother was not a model of virtue but a complex woman with a naughty streak, Erica felt safe to reveal her own closeted love life. The truth does set you free, and living in truth is a key component of healthy adulthood.

My own mother was always startlingly real. My fantasy mom belonged to my friend Rose. She looked like Angie Dickinson, rubbed my forehead, twirled my curls—and I never heard her shout. Decades later, I found out that Rose's mom was a wilted alcoholic whose daughter, her only child, didn't speak to her. This demise happened while my own iron-willed mother had survived the loss of her husband and the loss of her leg and prevailed, still doing her crosswords, still quick to criticize, but always there when a child needed her. Later, I will share details of my early playground envy and how I pitted Rose's mom against my mom. But the moral of this childhood delusion is the same one that holds for marriage: The grass is not greener on the other side; when the curtains are parted in the houses down the street, as they are about to be, your own imperfect mother will look pretty darned good.

Comparing mothers, like daydreaming about swapping mates, is a waste of time. For all you know, the mother who acts like a lamb may bang her kids with a skillet behind closed doors. The stories from Grace and Erica reinforce the necessity of focusing instead on accepting the actual woman who gave birth to you, the mother you are bound to by blood, DNA, and roots. She is your reality check. Letting go of the feel-good fantasy goddess and embracing your own mother is a shift that needs to happen as soon as possible, if you desire to live happily ever after, because your mother could be around for a very long time, given modern aging trends. She is an irrevocable fact of life.

You can ditch a spouse who turns from bad to abusive, but you cannot divorce your mother. You are stuck together until one of you dies. She will probably go first, and if unfinished business remains, you will be left embroiled in your own one-sided drama. The failure to complete and heal what is arguably the most important relationship in a woman's life can keep gnawing at a daughter's heart long after the funeral. Erica's poignant story later in the chapter illustrates this point. She speaks about the hard-earned closure she experienced just before her mother died, as each woman bared all while still capable of doing so. To maintain a peaceful heart while mourning a mother's death, we must lift the lacy veils of illusion now and start talking straight. Or, we can look forward to scenes like this one:

In Candace Flynt's 1987 novel *Mother Love*, three grown daughters confront their conflicted hearts about their difficult mother only after she has died—this after a lifetime of dancing around her. Here's a scene in which the daughters—Katherine, Jude, and Louise (nicknamed "Weezie")—are assembled in the cemetery, talking more openly and critically about their sharp-tongued, hard-drinking, sexually charged mother than they dared to do while she was alive.

"Stop it," Louise says shrilly. "We're in a graveyard. You ought to have a little respect. For God, if not for Mother."

"We're at our very own mother's grave," Jude says. "We're just being natural. We're talking exactly the way she would talk. You ought to try it sometime, Weezie. Stop always thinking about what you're *supposed* to do. Do what you *want* to do." She pauses. "God *isn't* here."

"You both make me sick," Louise says. Her cheeks are flushed; her eyes accusatory. Accusing them of being too much like their mother, Katherine thinks. Which, perhaps, they are, Jude especially. "I don't want to argue," Louise continues. "We're standing on her grave."

"Not *on* it," Katherine says.

"Yes, we are . . . She's here. Under our feet." With the growing dark, the sense of graveyard has become stronger. Louise thinks that if there were tombstones her sisters might be more reverent.

Katherine's face suddenly brightens. She stretches informally, ending the gesture by placing a hand on each sister's shoulder. Neither of them relaxes under her touch. "She's not under our feet. She's right here with us," she says, looking pointedly at both expectant faces and adds: "No, she isn't." She grins with the knowledge that they all share: "If she were here, nobody would be having any fun."

Louise steps away so that Katherine's hand drops off her shoulder. "Why do you always cut her like that?"

"I'm not cutting her. Look, Weezie, this is what we decided. We aren't going to rosy her up. We're going to remember her as she was. No purple haze . . . It's not disloyal." Katherine's voice becomes husky. "We're her daughters. If we're going to spend time remembering, we should remember her for how she was. She was a pain in the ass."

This passage is plucked from Candace Flynt's fiction, but in the dozens of real stories about real mothers compiled for this book, "pain in the ass" was a common assessment. There were very few mothers who matched this angelic description in Carl Jung's *Aspects of the Feminine*: a woman who is "lovingly tender, joyous, an untiring giver of solicitude and sympathy." That is, until I met Annette, a woman in her mid-fifties bestowed with a mother who is an angel, and this one didn't come from a television show.

I befriend Annette while waiting in line to board a flight at Baltimore-Washington International Airport. She has perfect blond hair, a perfect smile, and the perfect shawl draped around perfect shoulders. I tell her about the book I am researching on daughters growing old with their mothers. Her face beams and her voice dips into a worshipful whisper as she describes the perfect mother—her own, a woman who is about to turn ninety.

"My mother is the most giving woman in the world. I have nothing but wonderful memories," she says. I tell her that I am thrilled to meet her, because she is the first midlife daughter I have encountered thus far who seems to have no gripes.

She shakes her head and her expression is incredulous. "I can't believe that! I feel sorry for any daughter who doesn't totally love her mother." Before you read on and start pitying yourself, know this: Annette's mom is the only perfect mother I found in more than one hundred interviews with women of all backgrounds, rich, poor, black, white, gay, straight, ages thirty-four to seventy. They spoke of mothers with all sorts of quirks and personalities, from weak to stoic, manic to violent. Yet, the composite take-away from conversations that often went on for hours is that it is not the norm to feel "totally" one way, as Annette does. It is normal to fluctuate between emotions, from love and wonder to annoyance to sputtering outrage. It is normal to say, "I love you" and "How could you?" during the same day, even during the same dinner. Yet, most of us know at least one Annette, the friend who does have it all in a mother. Her mom is the type who fans unrealistic expectations—thus jealousy—because she is proof that somewhere perfection does exist. Annette has the gold-standard mother who comes not from a Brothers Grimm fairy tale but from a real house in a middle-class Midwestern town, where a family of three sisters went to Catholic schools, in uniforms laid out daily by a woman of pure goodness.

Annette's Story

My mother was always very loving and kind. She wanted religion to influence our education, so she made sure we went to Catholic schools. My mother didn't work, and my father was the Midwest sales manager for an aluminum company. Her work was her children.

She was always doing motherly things; she did homework with us, baked sweets for us, she made sure our school uniforms were laid out each morning. At night, she prayed with us and tucked us in. She was always in a good mood; nothing seemed to upset her. I thought everybody's mother was that way. My mother was never in my face about what I was doing. It was always easy to talk to her.

I remember, growing up, I would go up to her bedroom and she would be ironing. I would sit on the bed close to her while she worked, and we would talk about school, my friends, boys, about everything. I just assumed everybody else's mother was as good as my mother. She never overstepped her boundaries, even when I made choices she didn't necessarily agree with.

My husband is not Catholic, and he's from a divorced family. But my mother loved him and accepted him from the beginning. As I grow older, I couldn't have a more loving, more generous friend in my mother. We sit at the breakfast table and we talk and talk, like we did when I was a child, when she was ironing and I'd be sitting on her king-size bed. We talk about anything and everything, and even at ninety, she is very sharp. My father died three years ago, and my mother handles all her own checks and finances. She has never been a burden for us.

There's nothing more I need to say to my mother: Our relationship is totally complete. I know that when she dies she is going to be with God and with my father. I know that I've been the best daughter and supporter I could have possibly been and that she's been the best mother she could have possibly been. I'm telling you, there was never a cross word between us.

Hmm, never a cross word? The image of a mother and daughter cooing at each other constantly makes me feel really crummy as I remember the "F—k you!" showdown with my own mother in the driveway a couple of years ago. Although I never clung to the illusion that mine was the perfect mother, many women I spoke with did recall periods of idolization when they were children. Annette is still locked in childlike awe, but for most women, such reverence vanishes over time. As we age, we usually end up seeing our once-formidable mothers stripped down to their naked selves, as needy of us as we once were of them. This can be a debilitating transition for both mother and daughter, each accustomed to independence. Annette's mother has never been in a hospital, except to give birth. Will her mother fade placidly and give her family a fairy-tale ending? Or, will her daughters be burdened with an arduous deathwatch? Will Annette fall apart when her mother dies?

These prospects are frighteningly real for Grace right now. She leads us through her harsh reconciliation, as she watches her mother change from an unconquerable domestic queen to a sad and sickly widow.

Grace's Story 🍃

Grace is a forty-seven-year-old private investigator, raised by an all-competent, high-energy emergency-room head nurse. Her seventy-two-year-old mother is now retired and in dismal health, after multiple surgeries: knee, sinus, and most recently bladder. She is sad, impatient, and "a pain in the ass," says Grace, echoing the sisters in the novel *Mother Love*.

Sipping Jack Daniels, Grace sits at a picnic table on the screened porch of her cabin on the edge of a pine forest in Delaware. The air is muggy from an afternoon thunderstorm, and the only sound is the drum-rattle of cicadas. Grace wears a chalk-blue V-neck sweater and no makeup. Her red hair is short and gelled into spikes, and large silver hoops glisten at her ears, a birthday present from her mother. "She buys me great gifts," says Grace, touching her earrings and staring into the trees.

Grace's "pioneer woman" mother taught her seven children in New Mexico how to use every tool in her toolbox and even how to construct their own homes. On this damp day, Grace sadly reflects on watching "Superwoman" morph into a defeated, dependent woman. "She was my fantasy mom growing up; being around her now can be a nightmare. I would never have expected her to turn out this way."

The daughter is now the nurse, often sleeping in the same bed with her mother. Grace compares this caregiving to when she had babies. "All I can do for my mother is just love her and hold her and talk to her when she wakes up in the middle of the night."

Grace's account of a supremely powerful mother who comes tumbling down and the daughter who is there to catch her reveals two women who must submit to a large dose of reality and colossal pain. While Grace is coping with something many adult daughters face—the role reversal from child to caregiver—she is also reassessing her mother's entire personality, finding that Superwoman is just human.

Look, I know that there are truly horrible mothers out there, and I don't really have anything to bitch about. But it's hard for me to watch "Superwoman" lose her power. Now I see this aging woman in failing health, and she is so depressed. Her depression has taken the form of anger: anger about her illnesses, anger about the world. She bitches about everything and lashes out at her children and makes us all miserable.

She was Superwoman my whole life: doing a hundred things at once, very positive, always very demonstrative with her love, hugging and kissing us all the time. I would never have expected her to react this way to adversity, and it is very disappointing to me. I don't understand it; and I'm frightened by it. Because I am afraid that if she, who was so much, could be so diminished—I will end up the same way.

My mom was an enviable and envied mom, one of those moms the other kids wanted as their mom. They would con-

fide in her, and they would hang around our house. She worked full-time as an ER nurse, yet she made us a beautiful home on a small budget. She had the greatest laugh, the greatest energy. She was just so easy. You could talk to her about anything and she listened. She was always available. My friends thought she was fascinating.

My parents married young, and they were both forty-six when my father died of a massive heart attack. He got tuberculosis as a soldier in the Korean War, then ended up in a hospital in the Midwest, where my mother worked in her first position as a nurse. He was supposedly dying; the doctors had to remove one of his lungs and gave him three months to live. Against medical advice, our mom brought him any food he wanted, thinking you had to grant a dying man his every wish. They married at twenty-one and had seven children in the first ten years of their marriage. He lived for another twenty-five years, with one lung, working as an architect and builder—but always propped up by our mother.

He wasn't a ball-throwing kind of dad. But our mom was like a man in her physical strength, though she is very petite. She built things—furniture, stairs, patios, additions to rooms. There was no power tool made that she couldn't master, and she used a glue gun like a weapon. Strangely, I never saw my father, the builder, with a hammer in his hand. She was that kind of woman, the kind who can do anything. She was Superwoman before that term was used to describe a woman who could do it all. My mother had an enormous impact on me and on all my siblings. I became very much like my mother in some ways, independent and overachieving. Because of my mother, I have never met a power tool I didn't like.

Flashing back to a Supermom armed with power tools who turned seven children into confident carpenters suddenly overwhelms Grace. She drizzles more whiskey into her glass and starts talking about a couch her mother once made, "a massive black and white thing. It was amazing." Gazing at the pines, sturdy like her mother once was, Grace is crying softly. I am thinking of my own one-legged mother who was also sturdy as a tree but now is like the skeletal branches of November, reaching for her last sunlight before the barren, cold winter. Soothed by the lush landscape, a composed Grace recounts the second phase of their relationship, when her mother started to crumble.

So there we were, a happy family, my two sisters, four brothers, living in a great house in the mountains of New Mexico, and my dad drops dead. It was 1979 and I was twenty-three years old, living in Europe. My mother took it absolutely horribly. I thought she'd be brave, but she fell apart. It happened one night after dinner. Meals at our table used to be very long; we'd sit there for two or three hours, having really wonderful conversations. My mother would make a big pot of chili or goulash, and we'd eat and laugh and argue for hours. After one of these meals, my dad had a heart attack. My mother tried to revive him at home, but he didn't make it. There is no question for me that his death marked the beginning of the end of my mother as I believed her to be—funny and smart and sexy.

It took a really long time to get the news to me and for me to make my way home, but I remember thinking, "I will be OK when I see my mom. I just need to get to my mom." But when I got home, she wasn't there. I didn't know this woman. Here was my mother, curled almost fetally in a chair. I went to crawl into her lap, and instead she crawled into mine.

I thought, "OK, she needs me more than I need her right now." So we just kind of made the switch that day. We had been preparing our whole lives for our father's early demise. He wasn't supposed to live that long; he got twenty-five years that he wasn't supposed to have. And my mother knew that. When it happened, I was expecting her to say to me, "Oh honey, it's all right." But she wasn't like that at all. She was completely undone and inconsolable. And I became her mother, a role I am still sometimes asked by her to play today.

So, at twenty-three, I began to get disillusioned that my strong and perfect mother wasn't who I thought she was. I saw her weak and vulnerable. I really mothered her during the first months after his death, putting my own grief about my father on hold. Several weeks after he died, I felt like she was ready for me to leave. I returned to Europe with the understanding that my mother would come within a year and we would travel together. I figured that I'd have time then for her to become my mother again, to help me grieve. Several months later, she got off a plane in Lisbon with her boyfriend. I had never even considered the possibility that my mom might be dating.

It was an embarrassingly hot romance for me to watch. They were all over each other. They married soon after, and I'm happy to say they stayed together for the next fifteen years, until he, too, died suddenly of a heart attack. I wish I could say she became stronger with her new lover, but she became more self-centered. She was in love, and for the most part, she was done being a mother. She had been a wonderful mother, but then her mothering stopped at exactly the wrong time. After losing my dad, I needed her, but she needed something else.

But in fact, she did come through for me in a very big way later. When I wanted to leave my husband, she was really my advocate, and that freed me to make the hard move. I met my current husband during that time—we took a week-long writing class together, then I wrote him every day for three months. On that basis, I fell madly in love with him and moved to another country. It was like taking a kamikaze flight, moving in with a wonderful man I barely knew. And when I told my mother about it she supported me. She said: "I trust you. Do what you need to do." So, as it turns out, at another intense time of need, she was there for me.

It was terrible when her second husband died; she could really use him right now. Frankly, we all could. They were traveling the world and having a blast. He saved her. Then, just like with my father, he died in an instant. She was only sixty-one. My mother is a woman who needs a man. Not only was she heartsick, she became physically sick. Over the past few years, she had to have her bladder repaired, and she's had chronic kidney infections, a hysterectomy, failed eye surgery, debilitating arthritis. And here's this woman, a real "pick yourself up by the bootstraps" kind of mother while I was growing up, and she is a horrible patient. She's a really loud complainer, and as a nurse who knows every-thing, she hates all doctors.

But, you know, even when my mom acted powerful, I al-ways questioned her bravado. I always felt that underneath that "I can do anything" attitude was a very vulnerable woman trying to prove something. My mother was abandoned by her father, and she never got over that. I think that she meant to be both mother and father to her own children, so that we wouldn't suffer like she did. It is very difficult to see her body, and her emotions, deteriorate. She was vibrant and attractive, well muscled, sexy. Last time I saw her, I gave her a bath. And it was like bathing a baby; she was so diminished in size, so tender, so helpless. My mom used to be so outwardly happy. She loved her job, her husband, her children, her life. Now, she's in so much pain, everything inside of her hurts, and all of what was good is mostly gone.

I haven't seen her genuinely joyful in a very long time. It is hard to be happy when I know my mother is not. I may never again see my mother really laugh. But if she were to die tomorrow, I would feel complete in my love for her. My mother gave all of her children something very important: We are not afraid to face a blank canvas. We are not fearful about trying things. She is still amazing to me for giving us that gift. My six siblings all stayed close to home. I live the farthest from her, yet my mother would say I am the closest to her. When I visit, I sleep next to her, our legs touching, holding hands. We are so physically connected that I know I will feel it in my whole body the moment she dies.

Since I was a child, my mother has always said to me, "I don't know if you are my daughter or my mother." I am her daughter.

Grace's mother is shedding her Superwoman persona as she is weakened by widowhood and declining health. This can-do mama was once the envy of her daughter's girlfriends; now Grace envies girlfriends with self-sufficient moms. The transformation in her mother is excruciating and puzzling to witness, as it is for other adult daughters with fantasy-moms-turned-invalids. Even if your own mom is taut from Pilates and slicing up opponents on the tennis court, Grace's rite of passage may one day be your own story. When an uber-mother becomes incompetent, her daughter—while initially blind-sided—must adapt to the new reality and develop coping strategies. Grace's accommodation to the changes in her mother (be it begrudging at times) is an example for any of us thrust into a fantasy gone awry.

Erica's Story

Erica's mother went from victim to heroine, the opposite of Grace's turnaround. As she watched her Trinidad-born mom being slapped around by a sexist and belligerent husband, Erica perceived her to be a pushover. But the woman who revealed herself to Erica shortly before her death was actually bold and edgy in her choices in life and love.

In the last years of her mother's life, both women exposed their secret selves. Erica, thirty-six, opened up about her lesbian lifestyle about a decade ago, right before Thanksgiving, when she informed her mother she was bringing her lover—not a man—home to dinner. Her mother made her own astounding confession, which obliterated Erica's sense of identity and the fantasy that her mother was weak.

Erica is sprawled across an antique sofa of burgundy brocade in her living room in an apartment just outside New York City, where she works as a high school teacher. Her mother's indomitable Caribbean spirit pervades the room, captured in a glamour shot showing her dark, luminescent skin and eyes that crinkle when she smiles. Toying with the fat twists in her hair, Erica speaks of loving and losing a "buddy" who became, in her final years, the exemplary mom her girlfriends wished they'd had, just like Grace's mom was in her prime.

My mother, Cynthia, eloped shortly after World War II, at the age of seventeen, to marry a man seven years older who was very abusive. They were part of the small immigrant community from Trinidad that settled around New York City during the Harlem Renaissance period. She married when she was young to get out of her parents' house, which was also oppressive.

Her marriage was hard and unhappy, and she did not have children right away. Then, while she was married to this man, she met his first cousin, whom she fell in love with. My younger brother and I are really her children by this cousin, but my mother never told her husband. We found out much later, but basically we grew up thinking that the mean man she lived with was our real father, although our biological father was actually "Uncle Errol." I know it's complicated, but she kept this secret for a very long time. So we were raised in a tense environment by a man who believed we were his children. Later on, I wondered if his behavior was intensified by his suspicion of her unfaithfulness.

I remember hating my mother by the time I was eleven, because as I got older, the abuse became more severe, toward both her and her children. I hated her for living with this man. I wished they would get a divorce. I prayed she would take us away. I hated her for letting him make our lives so miserable.

When I did find out the truth years later, my mother said that what she wanted most in the world was to run off with her lover and take their children with her. But my real father didn't want to disrupt his cousin's family. So we were all living this big lie. Once I found out the truth, I started remembering that my mother would always take these so-called business trips to upstate New York when I was young, and she'd be gone a week or more. She later told me she was meeting her lover. When her husband died in 1993, she got back together with my biological father. They were both in their sixties when they were finally able to be open about their relationship, which had always been very romantic, very passionate. And they lived happily ever after until just recently, when he passed away. He waited for her husband, his cousin, to die before he would marry her.

I'm a snooper, very curious, and I used to pick through all of my mother's papers. After her first husband died, I was doing some serious snooping and found letters he had written, apologizing for breaking her fingers. He was truly violent. Mothers are supposed to protect their children and to stand up for themselves. But I did not go to my mother and yell at her for taking her husband's abuse. I never went whining to her. And when he slapped me, she wouldn't do anything. She would leave the room. Once, when he was nearly beating me unconscious, she told him to stop—and that was the only time she ever stepped in. I remember thinking as a child that living with this man was like living in a dictatorship. But, in my culture, men were the bosses of the family.

While she was married to this man, I thought she was very weak, which was very different from her public persona.

She was successful at her job, working for the Public Service Commission of New York. When she retired, she was a hearing officer, the highest non-appointed position you can reach in the commission, which regulates public utilities for the state. So, on the one hand, my mother was a positive role model. She had an impressive career. But then, she put up with this abusive man.

After he died and I found out who my real father was, I asked her, "Why in the world didn't you just leave this monster when you had someone nice, someone you loved?" She said she stayed because she thought he would be a better financial provider for us and that she didn't realize the abuse was that bad. When I brought up specific beatings, she said she didn't remember that happening. We're talking crazy amnesia, total denial.

Looking back, I realize that she exhibited classic signs of depression. I would come into the kitchen, and she would be sitting with her elbow on the windowsill, her chin cupped in her hand, just staring out the window. She gained a lot of weight, and she often looked really unhappy. Then, when her husband died, she completely changed.

She lost weight. She bought new clothes, really fashionable styles. Before, she dressed like an old matron. She started taking cruises and vacations, to Mexico and Hawaii. And she was happy. She was like a new person. It was an amazing transition. At the age of sixty-three, she became the mother I always wanted.

It was really wild for me. Imagine, here's this mother who is deeply depressed, overweight, and suddenly she has a sexy spark. Then, the guy I thought was my uncle started coming to the house. My mother tells me that she is seeing this guy romantically, and I'm thinking, "My mom is dating my uncle? This is weird!" And then he basically moved in.

I was always talking to my lover about this bizarre situation, and one day she said to me, "Erica, he's your father! You look just like him. Wake up!" She had put everything together. At first I thought, "That's impossible." But then I was like, "Duhhhh!" So one day, my life flipped over. I phoned my mother and demanded to know, "Is Errol my father?" And she said, "Yes, he is." It felt crazy, completely surreal. Everything I knew as truth wasn't real. Suddenly, at the age of twenty-six, my whole life wasn't what I thought it was.

I got very, very mad. Here I had a real father who was a good man, and instead I had to grow up with a violent father, who actually wasn't my father at all. It blew my mind! Then I began to find some humor in it, that my mother would dare to be so scandalous. My mother? She had always been such an ethical person, always followed the rules, never cheated on anything. And here she's living this huge secret life.

Erica had her own huge secret life. Although her brother and friends knew she was a lesbian, she was hesitant to tell her mother, afraid of rejection—or worse. She finally told her while she was a student at Georgetown University Law School, and her fears turned out to be unfounded. Many of her gay friends were rebuffed when they leaked their news at home. Yet, Erica's mother responded with love and curiosity, extending her maternal support to her daughter's wide circle of pals, many with mothers who had checked out of their lives. Her open reception only corroborated what Erica was starting to see when her real father's identity was revealed—that the woman who once appeared meek and malleable was really forceful and freethinking. Here's how the two women flourished after airing their truths:

I had known forever that I didn't have crushes on boys. I had crushes on girls. I wanted to be their boyfriend. And, contrary to what some people think, I did not become gay because of my experience of living with an abusive man. There were lots of men in my life who weren't abusive, especially lots of wonderful uncles in my extended family. My mother never said to me, "Why don't you have boyfriends?" She never pressured me to do anything. She always let me be. She thought I was great just how I was.

And I was a really good kid. The positive side of my mother did give me a lot of inspiration and support. Watching her succeed in a career made me want to succeed. I got great grades, always at the top of my class. I got a scholarship to Miss Porter's boarding school, went to undergraduate and graduate school at Georgetown. I never gave my mother any trouble. I had my first girlfriend when I was seventeen, and I kept thinking, "I gotta come out to my mom, I want to come out to my mom." I wasn't closeted anywhere else except around her. At twenty-two, I was living in Washington in an apartment with my girlfriend, and my mom called to see if I was coming home for Thanksgiving. I said, "You don't want me to come home, because you won't want to meet my date."

She said, "Whomever you bring, if you love them, I will love them."

I said, "Well, what if it's a woman?"

She said, "That's OK," and I just started crying hysterically. She said, "I thought you might be gay because you never had any boyfriends." She was just great about it. She would come to Washington, and my friends loved her. Many of my gay friends had coming-out experiences with their own mothers that were very hostile. So my mother became like a mother to them, too. I was very lucky to have a mother who was accepting of my gayness; there are so many parents who turn away.

Until we both came clean, I didn't really talk honestly with my mother. I would listen to her, but I wouldn't talk to her about how I was feeling. I wasn't myself with her because I didn't trust her. After we were both "out," she started to tell me things about her past, about trying to juggle her husband and a lover and her children. And I told her how I had been carrying around a lot of rage and sadness for a long time. I told her that I was so mad at her for tolerating the abuse. In this new light of truth, I was able to fully let her into my life. She began to hang out with me, go to women's festivals with me. We became buddies.

Seeing each other through this new lens, we had a rebirth throughout my twenties that lasted until she died recently. She accepted me as an adult. And I was able to accept her as someone who wasn't perfect, someone who had flaws, and that was OK. I came to see that my mother was unconditionally in my corner. When mother and daughter connect deeply, it's the best relationship a woman can ever have. I worked hard for it. My mother and I got a second chance; we had a "before" and a "happily ever after." After years of thinking she would never change, she did. She apologized to me. And I let myself be open to that. I grew, too. And this is the greatest gift my mother ever gave me—her beautiful, honest, loving self.

Her mother's death clearly rocked Erica, who says she is still overcome with grief. Yet she also feels "an incredible sense of freedom." Her mother died knowing the true Erica, and Erica, too, is left without any nagging questions. The connection is pure and eternal, not one tainted with regret. Truth is more important than perfection.

Erica's story makes me newly grateful for Helene Krasnow, who never pretended to be anything other than her imperfect self. But let me re-introduce my sixth-grade fantasy mother, who turned out to be a sham. Rose's mother could have snagged a Best Actress award for portraying a hip, happy housewife. Yet offstage she was lost and miserable.

I spent much of junior high being jealous of Rose's maternal fortune. Her mother not only looked like Angie Dickinson, she had a voice like Lauren Bacall's and a body like Barbie's. She was thirty-four when I met her, wore black miniskirts, hugged me whenever I came over, and drank whiskey sours at 5 P.M., dangling the cherry by the stem and slowly pulling it into her mouth with her tongue. I watched her, hypnotized, as if she were in a movie. I mimicked her moves in my bedroom mirror, imitating the way her mouth grabbed for cherries, how her slender fingers arched.

One morning Rose showed up on the school playground with a red skateboard, the first skateboard I saw glide eastward from California, purchased by her mother on a trip to Malibu. Rose taught the girls in our clique how to surf on the sidewalks surrounding Horace Mann School. I was envious that Rose lucked out with such a cool, young mother. Why wasn't my mom like this—trendy and engaged? Rose's mother paired black fishnet stockings with her black minis; my own mother, who was more than a decade older, wore a flowered apron over black stretch pants—the ones with stirrups at the feet.

This is the year that I—eleven and pubescent—got mad. Mad that my mother sat at the kitchen table most of the day, doing crossword puzzles, sullen, sighing, buried in herself. In the late afternoon I would often find her lying on the striped blue chair in the living room, head back, eyes closed, clutching a black-and-white photograph of her dead parents. Sometimes she would sit so still that I would crouch by her side to make sure she was breathing. When her chest barely moved, I would shout, "Mom!" and she would play dead and not answer me right away, which just made me more frantic and afraid. I think she actually enjoyed her little game, because seeing me so fearful was a validating rush of proof that I loved her.

As a child of a mother who perpetually mourned, I felt very old while I was still very young. Ancient Yiddish peppered her sentences, and her Polish-French accent was so thick that I would beg her not to talk when my friends were around. Rose's mother spoke in a lilting voice, was always smiling, and would grab my hands and ask about my day. I wanted Rose's mom: She could teach me how to be stylish, how to be a woman, how to be happy. At the time, my mother was nothing like who I wanted to be. She talked funny and loudly, did not advise me about clothes or sex, and generally seemed surly. I couldn't have slumber parties: too noisy, too many people to feed, too chaotic for a mother who was geared like a clock.

As a child in her house, my stomach hurt a lot.

But I'll take memories of stomachaches over what Rose ended up with as an adult. At my thirtieth high school reunion, several pals from my grammar school were there. They told me that Rose, the prettiest girl in our grade, had never married. Her parents were divorced. And her mom had turned into an alcoholic who was drying out in a clinic in Arizona. Those whiskey-soaked cherries that fascinated me were sexy, but they were poisoning her. While Rose's show-horse mom had taken an ugly turn, my own plow-horse mother had stayed the course, still dishing out biting commentary, but still irrepressible, still her original self.

My mother was not a fantasy that went *poof*. I could count on her to answer the phone when I called, to be at the door when I visited, to feed me when I was hungry, to make sure I was warm, to fight for my siblings and me. This is more than what many people get, I realize as I hear tale after tale of mothers who take three-hour naps and let their children fend for themselves.

As a child, I was angry that my mother was tough and uncompromising. I was often embarrassed by her brusque manner. Today, I am proud of her complete lack of self-consciousness and how suffering and loneliness don't scare her. She may be selfish, but she is also self-sufficient. She didn't teach me how to cook or how to primp for a date. But this mother of mine, who wasn't big on coddling, taught me the most valuable lesson of all: how to be resilient and to speak from my heart. When I started seeing my mother for who she is and stopped resenting her for who she could never be, we started to have a real friendship built on truth and resolution.

A month ago she came to Annapolis. On a Saturday morning, just after breakfast, she became sweaty and pale and fell into such a deep sleep that not even my son Zane, playing full-pedal *Tarantella* inches from her wheelchair, could rouse her. We thought she was dying. I called 911, and while I was speaking to the dispatcher, my mother woke up. She put her hands over her ears, grimaced, and began screaming about my "noisy house." I pressed my tear-streaked cheek next to her cold face and said: "Mom, thank God, you're alive. And I know you're OK. Because you're still a bitch." Years ago, that comment would have elicited her chilling wrath. But over this Memorial Day weekend 2005, my eighty-five-year-old mom, softened with senility, only gave me a wagging of an index finger and a sarcastic smile.

Grace and Erica know that they should count their blessings, too. Their mothers weren't A-plus in every category, like Annette's goddess mom. But, in the end, their imperfect moms got high marks in the right stuff: They were respectful, present, and loving. No one is all good—not me, not you, not our mothers. Letting go of youthful dreaming and surrendering to the grind of reality is essential to completing the circle of life, which often ends with a daughter mothering her own mother. The failure of our moms to live up to our expectations is captured in Nancy Friday's *My Mother/ My Self*, published in 1977, a pioneering book about mothers and daughters and anger and illusions. Here, Friday presents a scene from her imagination that, had it really occurred, she says could have "helped us both":

> In her kind, warm, shy, and self-deprecating way, mother calls me into the bedroom where she sleeps alone. She is no more than twenty-five. I am perhaps six. Putting her hands (which her father told her always to keep hidden because they were "large and unattractive") on my shoul-

ders, she looks me right through my steel-rimmed spectacles: "Nancy, you know I'm not really good at this mothering business," she says. "You're a lovely child, the fault is not with you. But motherhood doesn't come easily to me. So when I don't seem like other people's mothers, try to understand that it isn't because I don't love you. But I'm confused myself . . . I don't feel that serene, divine, earth mother certainty you're supposed to . . . ."

When Friday wrote *My Mother/My Self* more than twenty-five years ago, adult daughters turned it into a bestseller, raring to start anew. Yet, this urge to abandon the illusory and accept what is real came too late, just as many adult mothers were nearing their ends. The average life span for women back then was about seventy-six years. This early departure left little time for a daughter, barely into her own full-blown adulthood, to work maturely toward a relationship renaissance with her mother. As I write this book, women who remain free of cancer and heart disease can expect to live well into their eighties and beyond. This means that your mom could be showing up for dinner for the next twenty years. At this new plateau, made possible by advances in medicine and the rise in aerobic exercise for seniors, daughters at midlife have an extended opportunity to savor their imperfect mothers, ditching grudges and false hopes and pushing toward a relationship that is true.

It's a relief to have arrived at this point of light while my own mother is alive, as Grace and Erica were able to do. Now I can enjoy the narrowing window of her life, without avoidance and denial. I am struck by the shift in who I am when I'm around her. No longer holding out for what Friday calls "the mythic All-Loving Mommy," I now want to see my mom more often—this after too many years of bristling during our visits. Barreling through the vintage blocks of anger has allowed us to re-invent who we are together: I am a nicer daughter; she is a nicer mother who knows her end is near. If my mother dies tomorrow, I believe I will have Erica's balance between a grieving heart and a tranquil mind.

My mother once told me, "I did the best I could," when I rattled off my list of what she did wrong. I feel the same way. I am doing the best that I can to be a daughter who tries to show my mother pure love. I tell her now what I couldn't tell her growing up: that she did a fine job, and I feel lucky she was mine. The less you expect from your mother, the easier it is to be kind.

chapter three

EMBRACING
MOTHER DEAREST

To be completely present is to love.
To pay attention is to love.

—SHARON SALZBERG, *Lovingkindness:*
The Revolutionary Art of Happiness

W HEN I MOAN about my worries or my regrets, my
wise-man neighbor, seventy and pot-bellied, leans on
the fence in my backyard filled with orange lilies, smiles be-
atifically, and repeats his Buddhist mantra: "Don't dwell on
the past or the future. Let this moment bloom before you—
forever." *Nirvana*, that state of prolonged enlightenment, is
translated into English as "cooled" or "snuffed out," like a

candle's flame. Few followers of Buddhism are able to sustain this peak state in which the seeker is able to snuff out interference and be blissfully locked in the present. Yet lots of mindful daughters experience *satori*, Zen flashes of enlightenment, during visits with even the most jarring of mamas, by succumbing to the Ram Dass rule to *Be Here Now*. In his hippie guide to instant Buddhism published in 1971, Ram Dass advises us to focus on "centering, calming, extracting myself from the drama." In other words, flow, don't blow. Being here now means that when your mom is acting like a blustery drama queen and the veins start throbbing in your neck, you breathe deeply, hold the insults, act fifty not fifteen, and love the mom you're with.

Deep breathing must also be practiced for lesser crimes—when she tells you your kids are brats, your hair is too gray, or your clothes look cheap.

Loving-in-the-moment and snuffing out brain chatter does seem to ease the path toward a calming connection with moms who are pros at bringing on the jitters. Here are three daughters learning to relax in the face of varying degrees of tumult, from mild tremors to heart-quakes. They share their lessons on how to embrace Mother Dearest, even on her prickliest days. Although their lists of complaints range in severity from "she's annoying" to "she's poison," they have all arrived at the same hard conclusion: A mother's primal tug is a force her daughter cannot escape. They tell us to stop fighting and surrender, get close to her, observe, take it all in. Our mothers' actions are how we learn to be women and to be mothers, even if it means vowing to do the opposite of everything that was done to us. Our mothers are our professors.

As we listen to Rita, Rebecca, and Chynna, we hear voices tremble with sadness and lift with joy. Their mothers, like our mothers, are complex women who are not all good and not all bad. The serious and ambitious Rita is learning to stop judging her party-girl mom. Rebecca has become her mother's "life coach," teaching a lonely, angry woman who was never mothered herself to be gentle and hopeful. Chynna is starting to feel the warmth of Michelle Phillips, an "untouchable" mother who loved from a distance while she toured with The Mamas and the Papas and traveled with famous boyfriends like Peter Fonda and Jack Nicholson.

Rita's Story ✍

Rita is a fifty-year-old advertising executive who owns her own firm in Denver. Athletic and brainy, she ranks as the number two tennis player at her club and was the valedictorian of both her high school and her Ivy League college. It is 8:15 P.M., and she just returned to her home outside of Boulder after thirteen hours at the office, a typically long day that has helped pump her company's earnings up to $1.5 million last year. She wears a brown silk blouse, a beige Anne Klein blazer and carries an alligator briefcase.

Putting her briefcase on the counter, she rifles through the mail and then sinks into a suede sofa that swallows her sinewy frame. The sunset casts slits of light onto the gold combs that hold back a tumble of black hair. With her eyes fixed on the mountains turning mauve with dusk, she begins to describe her septuagenarian mother, a voluptuous blond who does the bars at night, devours mysteries, and could pass for fifty-five.

"She's the quintessential Power Granny," says Rita, the mother of two college students, a girl and a boy. That power is both "awesome and annoying," she adds.

Yet Rita unquestioningly understands the pressing importance of learning to tolerate all sides of her mother, because the females on that side of the family live past ninety-five. Her choice is clear: She can spend the next two decades being irritated that her mother is more unbuttoned party girl than buttoned-up intellect—like Rita herself. Or she can be entertained in the moment by an effervescent woman Rita calls "over the top."

My mother was a classic fifties housewife. She thoroughly cleaned the house every day. She cooked every meal. She was always home. As a child, I felt totally loved by her. But my mother was a nag, a nudge. She pushed me incessantly. She expected me to be the smartest, the best in the class. In those days, it was all about academics; girls were not involved in competitive team sports. And I did very well in school; I was the valedictorian of my class of four hundred students, and I landed at an Ivy League college. Yeah, my mother really drove me hard. I never got a B. I spent my youth trying to please her; how I appeared in her eyes was always too important to me even after I grew up. I needed to know that she was incredibly proud of me, and it wasn't always apparent.

She is very smart; she went to Radcliffe, and in those days, for a girl, that was a very big deal. She was very attractive, petite, buxom, thick blond hair, always dressed very fashionably, even though we didn't have a lot of money. Everything changed suddenly. When I was twenty-four, my mother was in the hospital having a hysterectomy. I came home from graduate school to help. I remember the operation was on a Wednesday, and while she was recovering from that, my dad checked into the hospital the following day, which was Thanksgiving. He had been in a lot of pain, and by that night, we knew it was extensive cancer. He died two weeks later. They were both fifty-five at the time of his death.

Some widows flatten out. My mother really surprised me; how she bounced back is nothing short of amazing. Here, she's this housewife my whole life, and suddenly the floor comes out from under her. Literally, it came out from under her; they had taken out a $50,000 home equity loan right before he died to renovate our house. I remember the walls in her bedroom had paint samples on them; the living room walls were coming down. Then he's gone, and who's going to pay for everything? They had spent a lot of money putting my brother and me through college, and me through graduate school. But my mother did fabulously. She immediately went to work in an architect's office. And at the age of seventy-seven, she still goes to work every day.

Soon after my dad died, she started going to bars at night. When I visit her, we walk into these places in her neighborhood and the bartenders all know her by first name. That used to infuriate me. More and more, I see that she wants to have a place to meet people and talk to people for an hour or so before she goes home to her lonely apartment. Basically, I used to refuse to accept her for who she really is. She loves history, and so in my judgmental mind, I thought she should take a history class at night and meet some fascinating, retired professor. She should go on one of those seniors' trips to Europe. She should read Tolstoy instead of mysteries. I wanted her to join a church and get in senior discussion groups and think deeply and meet a brilliant man. I mean, this woman went to Radcliffe! She should still be studying.

Well, that's over for me now, that feeling of wanting her to be different from who she is. I'm OK with the fact that she goes to bars after work and that her necklines are lower than I would wear. I'm through being upset that she dates men I would not date. This may not be the life I want, but it's her life and let her have it. Actually, I get a kick out of her now, and out of her youthful, wild side.

When I was in eighth grade, sneaking out to meet boys, she didn't ask and I didn't tell. I never talked to my mother about any of that stuff. Now the tables are turned: I forbid her to tell me about her dating life. I am able to enjoy my mother a lot more because I now set clear limits of what we can and can't discuss. Details about her boyfriends are definitely off-limits.

Yet, I encourage my daughter to talk freely. I ask and she tells. I was the one who took my daughter to get birth control pills the summer after freshman year in college. She came to me and said she was ready to have sex with a young man she had been dating for nine months. My mother never talked to me like that. But I am thankful because my ability to be open with my children is a direct consequence of our closed mouths on the subject. Yet, despite our stark differences, the mirrors are everywhere. My mother was so worried about everything. She wouldn't let us listen to the radio when my father was on a flight for fear that we would hear about his plane crashing. I've inherited some of her paranoia: I'm the one who hears sirens at night and thinks it's my kid in a car accident.

My mother pushed me and pushed me to excel in school. And maybe I push too hard. The other day my daughter came to me and said, "Mom, you expect too much out of me." And I told her what my mother always told me: "Work your hardest. Do your best. And you can become anything you want to be." I credit my mother with giving me the self-esteem to feel like I could, indeed, go after anything. So, yeah, there's a lot of good to embrace in my mother, along with what is annoying. She is definitely awesome. Once I had kids, I realized just how hard it is to be awesome all the time.

Her mother lived until she was ninety-seven, and so could she. Easily. She's very healthy now. And I have arrived at a place with her that I really want to create a deeper relationship built on trust and compassion. Part of it is that I want to set an example for my daughter of how you stand by your mother. When my grandmother was at her end, my mother was extraordinary in her care and love, and it's a lesson I will never forget. My mother became a really great daughter. I saw a side of her that astounded me, and I saw a glimpse of what I might need to do for her someday and hope I can do as well. I want my kids to know that I did my best for my mother.

We go to a horse ranch in Utah twice a year, and it's the place where I am the happiest, the most free; it's our escape. This is the first time we've invited my mom to come along. I know things are going to be fine, because she's only staying three days. Another trick that has turned our relationship around is that I am a firm believer that your mother's visits should not exceed seventy-two hours. She believes the same thing. In fact, she prefers the forty-eight-hour visit.

Even though our relationship has had conflicts, she's the one person who loves me unconditionally—even when it doesn't seem like love. My husband loves me to death—I know this and have known it since we started dating thirty years ago. But, hey, you never know how marriage is going to go, even in the best of relationships. You read stories of men who fall out of love with their wives, right? It happens. I know that my mother is never going to fall out of love with me.

Several years ago, we were having a glass of wine together, and she told me that recently she felt I hadn't been there for her. Rather than cringe and remain silent, I said: "Mom, with you I have a hard time knowing what you need or want from me. Can you tell me when you need help, so I can be there?" She didn't say much but surprised me the following week when she said that her therapist had told her that I should know what she needs. I wasn't happy with that reply, but it did make me more conscious of ways I could be there for her. A year later, right after her mother died, my mom said, "I just want to thank you because you have been really supportive of me throughout all of this." So I guess the lesson here is, ask and you shall receive.

In accepting her for who she was, it became easier to sense what she needed emotionally. In many ways, my grandmother's illness has been the bridge we needed. It was during this period of getting to really see my mother shine that I decided that I wasn't going to change this woman and that I didn't want to change this woman. I was going to love *her for who she is: over the top. Most importantly, I was going to start talking to her bravely and truthfully about my life and our lives as two adult women. The more I accepted that the clutter of our relationship is as much mine as hers, the more honest and loving I become.*

She could live as long as her mother did, so we need to establish this new relationship now. I will set limits and stick to them. I will enjoy her when I'm with her, quirks and all. You know, if the ending of a novel really blows you away, that's how you remember the book. I am working on writing those last chapters with my mom to make them great.

Historically, Rita's rub with her mother is more of a subtle friction than all-out abrasiveness. As she ages, the irritation is smoothing over as she stops judging her mom to be ditzy and frivolous and starts simply enjoying her. These two spry women, age fifty and seventy-seven, have a real shot to be girlfriends with a bond thicker than any other they've had.

When you start to not only love but to like your mother, you get to connect with a woman who really knows you, a woman who is you in many ways. And as Rita demonstrates, however different we may be from our mothers, the resemblance in the mirror becomes more distinct with each passing year. Rita's see-sawing emotions toward a mother who is as annoying as she is awesome are increasingly leveled as she mothers her own kids and realizes how hard it is to be awesome all the time. Her imposed limits on the length of visits are also shrewd. Every daughter knows that the burst of mother-euphoria can only last so long. Yet these days, when Rita is with her mom, they are truly together.

Rebecca's Story 🌿

Melding into oneness with the woman who gave birth to her isn't coming as easy for Rebecca. Her mother was far more than just "annoying." An Armenian immigrant, she tongue-lashed every member of her family in tirades that Rebecca recalls as "poison" to her childhood during the 1960s. Yet, she is managing to turn the other cheek and welcome her recently widowed mother into her family, hosting her for weeks at a time in her farmhouse in rural Amish country one hour from her mother's home in Philadelphia.

Rebecca's ability to transcend both rage and outrage and be civil comes from her bold promise to herself that she would let old poison be old poison. She is so bent on "shielding" herself from the blackness of childhood and not letting it darken the present that she refuses even to discuss the past with her mother. Rebecca's example is one any daughter harboring rage can grow from, as she shows how letting go of toxic memories keeps her from poisoning her own family.

Dented copper pots hang over us in Rebecca's sprawling kitchen in Lancaster County, Pennsylvania. We are seated on stools around an oak counter covered with recipes for a party her gourmet store is catering tonight. She wears black corduroy pants and a black cowl-neck sweater, which make her coal-colored eyes gleam like ebony. Smoking Marlboros and dabbing tears with a crumpled tissue, Rebecca, fifty-one, explains how forgetting, more than forgiving, has been her way of tolerating a hot-headed mother whose behavior has often been intolerable. Ironically, only by "putting up a wall between our emotions" has Rebecca been able to get closer to her mother.

My mother was angry about everything. She always felt like she didn't get her due. Then again, her life was never easy. Her mother died at childbirth, so she was wet-nursed all around the town. She left Armenia when she was eleven and became part of a poor immigrant class to settle around Philadelphia. She had to leave high school to go to work because her family needed the money. Then she married my father, but she was really in love with his brother—a relationship that obviously didn't work out. So as a young woman she was already angry—she was always wanting but never getting.

She really took it out on my father; she was always angry with him. My parents, sister, and I lived in a small house in a middle-class neighborhood, and the only reason we could afford to live there was because we lived with my father's parents and they provided the down payment. And my mother was angry about that, too. My parents had a horrible relationship—my mother always wanted him to be somebody else. She wanted him to be more. He worked picking vegetables on a farm. She didn't want to be living in his parents' house. My father was the sweetest, nicest man on the planet. He was the one who stopped his car to let someone else go. He was the one who helped the old woman to the grocery store. Everybody loved this man. He never said anything nasty to anyone; he would always turn the other cheek.

My mother was just contentious to the bone. My earliest recollections of going to grammar school were that anything could happen with her. If a boy threw a rock at me, she would go marching into our school and start screaming at the principal. Instead of going and speaking to his mother nicely, she'd pitch a fit to the whole school, screaming at teachers. *I was always so embarrassed. She cut a wide swath of enemies; where my father would see a friend, she would see an enemy. No matter where we would go, she would make enemies. She was always mad at someone.*

Then again, she worked hard, all day, in a lingerie factory. She came home at 6 P.M. and the fights began. She totally berated my father. He was castrated. He was humiliated. He was just constantly belittled and constantly hollered at. From the way he chewed his food, to the clothes he wore, to the way he shuffled his feet, to the haircut he got—every single thing—she picked on him. There was always screaming in our house. Awful screaming. She'd scream at my grandmother. She'd scream at my relatives over the phone. She'd scream out the window at the neighbors. I would get physically sick to my stomach. I was so skinny as a kid because she was always hollering, and I just couldn't eat. At night, my older sister would hold me because I'd be sobbing in my room, throwing up, because I couldn't stand the conflict.

I need to stop here and steady myself, as you might, too. The pain is searing, and some of it too familiar. I am recalling, as you may be, how a mother's shrieks can constrict a daughter's abdominal muscles to the point where she can't eat. Hearing Rebecca, the knot is back, in the middle of my lower ribs, the place where the emotions of grief and fear are first felt, burning like acid. Women who became too skinny or too fat from mothers who twist the knife with sharp language add their voices to the conversation in the next chapter. Because of the chaos of her girlhood, Rebecca is raising children who live and eat in a quiet house. Her story continues:

There is no screaming; first off, my husband wouldn't tolerate it. And because of how I grew up, I absolutely will not allow it. I can never be really close with my mother because of her rage. But after my father died two years ago, she has been around our house a lot; she stays for weeks at a time. My way of dealing with her is that I just put up a wall. I will not discuss emotional things with her. I will not discuss my father's death with her. Since I was a little girl and she was so mean to my father, I always said to myself, "She better not say nice things about him after he's dead," knowing she would. And now, this man she never had a kind word for her entire life, she talks about him like he's a saint. We'll be doing something with my kids, and she will say in a loving voice, "Oh, your father would have loved this." I can't talk to her about my father, because if I begin, I won't be able to stop. She cries every day about losing him, and I just walk away. She actually thinks he did this terrible thing to her— he left her alone in the world. I won't let her cry on my shoulder about him. That's my punishment. I'm not going to ever push through this wall with my true feelings because it'd be too painful. I am not going to say: "Why are you crying? You were horrible to him." I can't bear that conversation. She absolutely may not rewrite history with me. I know the truth.

I was so happy for my father when he died. My last words to him—I was holding his hand—were, "Dad, now you don't have to listen to her anymore." No more hollering. The only time I remember when they didn't fight was on Saturday nights when they went square dancing. As a child, I used to cry when I saw them dancing, because it was so nice to see them happy together.

And now when she comes down from her house in Philadelphia I can handle her, because I have put up that barrier. It's definitely easier to cope with her with that wall between us. I don't feel any compulsion to go deeper. I'm better off on my side. What's the point? What am I going to do? It's not like I can forgive her, because I can't, so I have to deal with her in my own way. I'm at peace with it. It's never going to be one of these cozy relationships.

My mom is an incredibly healthy eighty. What am I going to do with her for the next fifteen or so years? She will probably end up living here, even though our house is cramped. It terrifies me, but I am the one who must take care of her. I can't put her in an old-age home. When I was fourteen, I worked in a convalescent home, and I cleaned poop off old people and saw what went on—I can't put her there. She's my mother. I will be the one who will end up taking care of her. I have to. I want to. But I absolutely will not allow her to ever again be critical or yell. When she speaks to my daughter harshly, I tell her instantly: "Mom, don't talk to her like that. Kids don't respond when you yell." I should know. I can hear her screaming at me when I was a kid like it was yesterday. In the last couple of years, I have really started calling her on her anger. When my dad was alive and she'd be over here screaming at him, I'd say: "If you want to speak to Dad that way, it's your business. But don't do in front of my kids. Your grandson is upstairs crying because of your screaming. Stop." It really woke her up.

When I was a child I never confronted her. I never questioned her; she had enough problems working in a factory, and we never had enough money. Now I question her all the time. I spend so much of my time teaching her how to behave. I tell her flat-out what is acceptable. When she complains about being lonely, that "nobody ever calls me," I tell her maybe it's because she has alienated everyone around her. I suggest that she should take a pot of soup over to someone who has been her friend for forty-five years and try and patch things up. I'm turning into her life coach. I wish I had the courage to have these conversations with her earlier. I wish I had been brave enough to tell her: "Mom, you shouldn't speak to your husband that way. Why do you start fights with everybody? Why?" I wish I had pushed her when I was young. But I never did. I was terrified of her.

Today, I am fearless. And because we're playing by my rules, I like having her around. I like showing her nice things she never had, good restaurants, the theater. I like buying her clothes. And when she starts her self-pity widow routine, I just keep pushing her back into this moment, right here, and tell her: "Look, Mom, at all the good things you have. Healthy children. Healthy grandchildren. So what if you have a sore hip? At least you have both legs." And then I push her out the door.

We go out and do things; we don't have heavy talks. Having the wall up between us saves us both. I just don't have the head for hashing and rehashing what went wrong, to get lost in psychobabble. It would kill her to know I felt this way. When all is said and done, I have a great life. I love my work and I love my family. I am raising children who are very close to me, because I don't criticize them. My house is calm. Dealing with my mother has been a learning experience.

Yeah, it was really awful growing up listening to her scream at the top of her lungs and watching my father disappear into a turtle shell for my whole life. But it is what it is. I could choose to wring my hands and say, "Wasn't my childhood terrible?" But instead, I got out of there as fast as I could, and I used her as example of what I don't want to be. And she has mellowed. She was always like this caged gorilla just trying to break out, fighting, fighting. I think she's getting tired of fighting, but every now and then she'll get up and throw a few punches.

I don't think about "I need to forgive her." Forgive her for what—everything? I'd rather try and forget the worst and know that I benefited from adversity. Adversity is a good thing. Blame is such a useless emotion. I enjoy her for what she is, and when she gets negative I say, "Keep your mouth shut." I'm telling you—I'm her life coach. My living fear used to be that I would turn into my mother. Everything she did, I would do the opposite. Any advice she gave, I would do the opposite, unless it was about cooking. I fought very hard to be nothing like her. But as I get older and my children are getting older, I feel lucky to have her. Like anyone, you have to take the good with the bad. I've learned to shield myself from the bad.

I must say, recently things are much better. I am having my mom here this Thanksgiving, and in my prayers I will give thanks for many things. Wonderful children. A spectacular husband. And anti-depressant drugs. Because since my mother has been on them, she is a new person. Happy, positive, and easy to be around. How different her life would have been—not to mention my father's—had we discovered this sooner.

What's good is that my mother's Armenian traditions are so strong, and I am passing this heritage on to my children. I am inspired by her. My mother is a workhorse; there is no job beneath her. She'll get on all fours to wash a floor at the drop of a hat. And I am like my mother in that way. I see now that, while she was hollering, she was also a good mother. I remember every Saturday morning she'd go into our dark basement and make me new clothes, in the latest styles. She was an expert seamstress, and she could whip up anything. I always had the most beautiful clothes, the best ski jackets, the best dresses, the best skirts. When I think of my mother, I will always think of her hands. She was always cooking wonderful meals or sewing or doing something with her hands. She has beautiful, strong hands. I believe she was given those hands because she really wants to help people, but she never had the necessary tools to do things gracefully, and in a proper way.

She never learned some basic things in life. She was never mothered, so she never had any of the right women role models. And now I am helping her. That's my job now. But I always look at my hands and think: "These hands are not beautiful. I will never have my mother's hands."

I look at my own calloused hands, with long fingers and large veins, "farm hands," my husband calls them. Rough from water and soap and children and time, they are just like my mother's. While Rebecca doesn't see her mother in her hands, they hold the same power as all mothers' hands, starting with the matriarchs of the Bible. A mother's hands can build a House of Horrors or a House of Peace. A mother's fingers shape this moment with her children and their destiny, by cooking, slapping, stroking.

Rebecca's iron resolve to "shield" herself behind a wall reminds me of the Stoics of ancient Rome, who preached that only by separating from our intense emotions could we find clarity of mind and the ability to really love. She refuses to press her mother to rehash her transgressions or to analyze what went wrong and wallow in resentment. Instead, she endures her mother by keeping her at an emotional distance, and although her brand of love isn't tender or nostalgic, she is still right there for her mom, pushing her to be hopeful and alive, coaching her into a better life.

Her choice to embrace a woman who wounded her could not have come without a clear separation of her heart from her head. Rebecca realizes that "blame is a useless emotion" and that it's sufficient to forget if you can't bring yourself to forgive. Erecting a safety wall between them has given her the confidence to tell her mother, when it is warranted, "Keep your mouth shut."

In contrast, singer-songwriter Chynna Phillips desires nothing more than to see the walls come tumbling down. She's had enough distance to call it "abandonment." While Chynna's mother, Michelle Phillips, was touring with her band The Mamas and the Papas or traveling with boyfriends like Peter Fonda and Jack Nicholson, Chynna was cared for by her housekeeper, Rosa. Chynna's late father, also a member of the band, lived in New York. At thirty-seven, Chynna is reviving her relationship with her mother, who at sixty-two is slowing down, acting in television shows, and becoming Chynna's "fascinating" new girlfriend.

Chynna's Story ✤

Chynna is seated in a trailer parked in the Greenpoint section of Brooklyn, on the production set of a television pilot that stars her husband, actor Billy Baldwin. She cradles three-month-old Brooke in her arms, while three-year-old Vance and five-year-old Jameson tug at her khakis. The children all have Chynna's delicate features and white-blond hair. Chynna wrote to me in 1997 after reading *Surrendering to Motherhood*, the book I wrote about tailoring professional lives to adapt to childrearing.

At the time, Phillips was a childless newlywed, and she shared her "dream of having lots of kids and working out of my house so I can stay home with them." In that note penned eight years ago, Chynna also expressed how she wished her mother had "taken the time to stop what she was doing and take a moment to really see her daughter." On a cold March morning in 2005, Chynna says that time has come. The two accomplished Phillips women are now embracing a new relationship fueled by their shared passion for the Phillips-Baldwin children, for music, and for each other. Other dreams for Chynna have also come true. Since her chart-topping trio, Wilson-Phillips, disbanded, she has been able to become a mother who works from home, playing the piano and writing songs. She also has created something she never had growing up: an intact family and a sense of home. Here, Chynna speaks of the challenges of giving her children what she longed for as a child.

My first feelings I had about my mom were that she was a goddess. She seemed very untouchable to me as a child.

She was always very busy with her career and with her boyfriends and with her other passions. My mother and father divorced when I was two years old, so I don't have any recollection of them being married. Although I have half-brothers and half-sisters, I was alone a lot growing up.

Enter Rosa, our Mexican housekeeper, who I came to love as you would love a mother. My mom hired Rosa to work for us when I was very young. Rosa not only woke me up in the morning, but she got me dressed, made me breakfast, walked me to school, made lunch and dinner, bathed me, sang to me, put me to bed. And Rosa did not leave until I was nineteen years old. This woman had a deep commitment to me and to my mom. She was very demonstrative, which was very important for me as a child. She would hug me and hold me close and give me the little touches and kisses a child needs. I absolutely felt mothered by her.

Five years ago, my mom called and said, "Rosa died." And literally, I felt like a baseball bat had just hit me hard in my stomach. All the air came out of me. I couldn't breathe. I cried like a baby. Then I lit a candle, and the rest of the day was extremely peaceful. Rosa was a very religious woman, and I felt like I had connected with her spirit. She was very instrumental in introducing me to Jesus Christ, which completely changed my life. Because of Rosa I became a Christian, and that has been my salvation.

So as a child, I didn't think to myself that I should be getting more from my mother. I had plenty of love and caring from Rosa. You know, maybe I was in denial. But I didn't really question it; I just figured my mom is really busy and I'm getting what I'm going to get, and I'm not going to get anything more. Looking back, I must have been in tremendous pain, which is why I became so vulnerable to drugs, and why I eventually turned to drinking at a very early age. I found comfort in drugs and alcohol. Although I've had that under control for twenty years, at the time they helped me have a false security and feel accepted by my peers. When I was high, I didn't have to look at the emotional abandonment I was feeling. I mean, God bless her, I did love my mother. But it felt like I was just a secondary thought to this very exciting life she was leading.

I was very, very lonely. I remember sitting at breakfast every morning, and I would be waiting for the bus to take me to school. I was sitting there by myself, eating pancakes, and I was just very sad. I would feel this pit in the bottom of my stomach. The Aunt Jemima syrup would be on the table. And I used to imagine that Aunt Jemima, this big, warm, smiling woman on the label, would come alive in our kitchen and take me away. And she would become my mother.

My relationship with my oldest daughter is actually very challenging for me because of my childhood. It's hard to be able to openly adore her and give her kisses and tell her how wonderful she is and how smart she is. Of course, I do it, but it's sometimes scary for me. I believe the reason I struggle is because I didn't get much of that as a child. I never had a warm mother-daughter bond, and I'm so afraid of the relationship. I'm so afraid of giving her the love that I never received—what if I don't get it back? But I do it anyway, and I am working on feeling more comfortable as a mother. I know I can be better at it. It's not my daughter's fault; she is a sweet and beautiful and loving child. But because of the experiences I had growing up with my own mom, I'm afraid of having an intimate relationship with my own daughter.

Basically, it's just a role reversal. I mean, when I get close to my daughter, it's actually me getting closer to my own mother. It's healing the wound inside of me. And I have been able to get closer to my own mother over the years, and it's because I had kids. She's in a place in her life now where she is actually able to love and to be there. She is very proud of me and my family. We have both grown up. As I've matured, I am able to have compassion for her and to embrace her as a fascinating woman with challenges of her own. I stopped expecting her to be Aunt Jemima a long time ago. The interesting thing is, when I let go of those expectations, she started becoming more maternal. She visits us on the East Coast and just loves her grandchildren and dotes on them.

And I do go out of my way to be as warm and demonstrative and loving as I can be to my children; I think about what Rosa did for me. As a grown woman, I see now that the way you were mothered is absolutely all-encompassing when it comes to its effect on how you mother. I see that people either repeat the same patterns, or they do the exact opposite. And I made a choice with my own children that I would do my best to break the chain of abandonment and dysfunction, and I think I'm doing a pretty good job at it. My kids know I'm there for them. I am a very physical mother.

I think some people are scared of their children, scared to love so much. A big piece of the puzzle is that my mom's mom died when she was only five. She was never mothered. So she doesn't know how to do it. But, you know, she's really learning with my children. I have two girls, and I've already made the decision that I'm going to work hard at not allowing myself to play these mother and daughter tug-of-war games. I owe them that.

You know, sometimes, I look at my five-year-old girl and I say to her, "I love you." And she looks at me with an expression that just breaks my heart, and I think to myself: "Was she not expecting that from me? She seems caught off guard by those words." Yet, when she hears "I love you," everything about her little face softens. I do not remember moments like that with my mom. It was mothering at a distance. It was her show, not our show.

Yet, I know she cared. She put a roof over my head. I went to good schools. And she paid for everything, all by herself. She took me all over the world, to China, to Egypt, all over Europe. Actually, my mom wanted to call me Asia. My dad said, "Well, then we may as well name her North Vietnam or China." And my mom said, "China, oh, that sounds very good." My father had his downfalls—I mean, major problems. He became a heroin addict. But the one thing John Phillips had was that he knew how to stop his world and just be with me. He knew how to take a walk on the beach and hold my hand and be with me in that moment. He knew how to sit at the piano with me and say, "Let's write a song together." I absolutely credit him for my musical ability; my mom is a very good singer and songwriter, but she didn't know how to do that—how to stop.

My father loved kids; he really got off on being around kids, laughing with kids. That's what kids want. I am getting a lot better at stopping my world to be with my children. I am always around my kids. But there's a big difference between being with your kids and really being in the moment with them. Although I have this memory of being abandoned, as a young woman I've always had a deep desire to make children and family a priority.

We live in a great house outside of New York City. I feel like I'm part of a family for the first time in my life. My husband comes from a large family, and he knew what this feeling was like. But I have never known what a family truly felt like, or the depth of what a family means, until now. This is not what I had, but it is what I've been able to create.

For the first time in my life, I am home. There was this surrender after Brooke was born, and I was like, "Oh I get this." I am their mother, and it is up to me to make this a home. And I did it. These are my kids, this is my tribe. And we are settled. This is new for me. I went to fifteen different schools when I was growing up. My mom had a new boyfriend every couple of years.

My mother and I have a long way to go, and I am excited about the process. There are things I want her to know that I've never told her. I want to tell her how sad I am for her that she never had a mom. I want her to know how sorry I am that she didn't have that experience, because she suffered so much. I'm in a really good place right now with her. I can go to her and cry, which I was never able to do before. I am happy for that.

I mean, she is my mom.

Because of her mother, Chynna was driven to make a home and fill it with children—who have a fascinating grandmother. Because of her mother, Rebecca doesn't scream. And because of her mother, Rebecca's hands are wondrous with food, and she has the skills to run a gourmet food company. Because of her mother, Rita changes from her tailored suits into jeans and goes to bars to drink and laugh with bawdy widows.

Because of our mothers, we are good and we are bad. We may leave our mothers, but the essence of our mothers never leaves us. We are inexorably, forever joined.

It is only our mothers who can make us whole, even if they shattered us years ago.

I revisit the core principles of Buddhism, which pave the way for the Mother Embrace: The Buddhist belief is that human life is filled with suffering because of our tendency to want what we don't have. By releasing those cravings and seeing what is real, we move into feelings of surrender and compassion. In the end, it is a swelling of compassion, even the act of feeling sorry for a mother who is lonely or sick, that brings a daughter back home. This is certainly true in my case.

"Compassion does not seek to avoid difficult situations, nor does it desire that people be 'let off' lightly," writes Carole M. Cusack, in *The Essence of Buddhism*. "It involves the firm and unflinching acceptance of situations as they truly are, and seeks the solutions to problems with realism and determination."

In Herman Wouk's 1955 classic *Marjorie Morningstar*, the titillating portrayal of a young girl coming of age, there is a scene when fifteen-year-old Marjorie has caught her mother listening in on a phone call with her twenty-year-old boyfriend. Incensed, Marjorie confronts her mother with, "I wonder whether you know that people don't listen to other people's phone conversations?"

To that, her mother responds: "I'm not people. I'm your mother. You don't have anything to hide from me, do you?"

We all try and hide from our mothers, as teens and as grown women, but they find us. They know who we are. I am one of those daughters who dodges her mother's radar, but I always return. Because wherever I am, I am drawn back to her, as if she is my center. As I write our remaining chapter and try to make it great, I am totally awake in this moment and grateful I've had my mother this long.

"The older we get, the easier it is to embrace our mothers, even the tough mothers," says Ellen Baker, a Washington, D.C., psychologist whose own mom is eighty-two. Baker specializes in developmental issues and eating disorders in adult women.

"It is a gift that many women over fifty still have their mothers," continues Baker. "As we age, we are more able to see our mother as a whole person, including her strengths above and beyond her limits and dysfunction, past and present. We have lived long enough see our mothers grow up themselves, to become more gentle and compassionate. This can help counterbalance some of the hurt and pain that a mother may have caused, often unwittingly, as a younger, less-developed person.

"This is tremendously exciting, positive news. In effect, this potential extended passage in the human growth cycle allows mothers and daughters more time to 'get it right,'" she adds. "A good number of my patients are talking about how the mother they had as a teenager is not the mother they have at fifty. The bonus of a mother's increased longevity gives a daughter the added opportunity to heal the wounded self of an earlier time."

It is a chilly morning in late July, and I am seated on a mossy rock at the edge of the water at Raquette Lake Camp in the Adirondacks, where I spend summers directing the media program. My cold fingers are laced around a hot mug of coffee. Mist rises through the coral of dawn in front of

West Mountain, making the pine-covered hills appear surreal and undulating, like the waves. Yet, I am unable to lose myself in this luscious scene that seems painted by Georgia O'Keeffe, because mornings, unfailingly, make me think of my mother in her kitchen. She's an early riser like me, and I know she is drinking her first cup of coffee while I am drinking mine. She is wearing a flowered apron and starting a crossword puzzle, having finished her soft-boiled egg smeared onto buttered rye toast.

During visits to Chicago, I love the ritual of morning coffee with my mother, perhaps our most connecting tradition. Sipping her brand, which is also my brand, Folgers, at 7 A.M., we are both effusive and expectant about the virgin day. It is too soon for either of us to have misbehaved; the air between us is fresh and clear. We are fully present, our faces close together. The conversation is caffeinated, intimate, and kind. I'm checking out her wrinkles and she's checking out mine. Lake Michigan mesmerizes with its Windy City dance outside her window.

I try hard to re-create this morning rush of coffee-klatch love when I'm with her in the afternoon or at night and something is going on that threatens to push me from mindfulness into madness. Embracing Mother Dearest does come more effortlessly with the practice of loving in-the-moment, an art that, when mastered, means grown girls like us can turn our headstrong mothers into tame soul sisters.

Taming the tiger is not for the meek and doesn't happen all at once. It takes going back into the cage, time and time again. Mothers, even the snarliest ones, deserve a second and fifth and millionth chance. You gotta do it, because, as Chynna would say, "I mean, she *is* your mom." Those six words say everything about the primal wrench in the gut that propels us back to the source of our life. To know ourselves, we must get close enough to know our mothers, no matter how painful the trip back can be or how sharp the pain was that drove us away. The women in the next chapter on rage and resolution show us how to travel even the toughest roads back home.

chapter four

LOVE, RAGE, AND STOMACHACHES

*It was easier to have a relationship with food than
to try and have a relationship with my mother.*

— PSYCHOLOGIST ELLEN BAKER

A T THE AGE OF FIFTEEN, Ellen Baker soothed her sadness about a cold mother with the contents of a girlfriend's refrigerator, systematically attacking the goods within, "shelf by shelf." That afternoon in 1960 "marked the first official day of my lifelong crazy relationship with food," says Baker, fifty-nine, now a prominent Washington psychologist who specializes in female eating disorders. "When I tell clients 'I feel your pain,' I really mean it." Indeed, she is intensely familiar with the compulsion to splurge on sweets when the hunger for love isn't being satisfied. After decades of obsessing over numbers on the scales, Baker is learning to halt the killer routine of bingeing and starving and is beginning to turn inward for sustenance and nourishment.

Baker's arduous journey toward wellness and self-sufficiency has been expedited by opening up to her mother, a repressed woman raised on a farm in Ohio during the Depression. This rigid Germanic woman used to leave the room when young Baker even hinted at subjects that were emotionally charged or risqué. Today, in her mid-eighties, she has evolved into an important ally as her daughter confronts frightening hurdles in her marriage—engaging in frank discussions about intimate feelings and sexuality.

Baker attributes her craziness with food to an early "rupture with my mother," a sentiment I've often heard from women battling eating disorders. Over the course of a twenty-five-year journalism career, I've interviewed lots of daughters who have instantly, almost unconsciously, placed hands on their bellies when asked to describe their mothers. They blame these women who failed to feed them with affection as the culprits who made them too fat or too thin or just plain sick to their stomachs. It is clearly our abdomens, the core of our beings, where emotions hit us first and hardest; the flutters from love, the jolts from fear, the knots from grief, the acidic unrest that comes from rage. Food is sometimes our best revenge and our only friend. Plagued by emotional famine, we feast on physical treats.

In 1988, as a reporter at UPI, I interviewed Barbara Bush over tea in the vice president's residence on Massachusetts Avenue. With a dramatic roll of her bright blue eyes, she joked that "George eats whatever he wants and stays lean, but what I eat goes right here," and she patted her hip. When the conversation turned to her upbringing in Rye, New York, Bush said she was "a very fat child" with a mother who loaded the table with buttery mashed potatoes and served real cream with cereal—but poked at her daughter during meals.

"I spent all my life with my mother saying, 'Eat up Martha' to my older sister and, 'Not you, Barbara,'" remembered the former First Lady. "That's the way I think of my childhood at the table. Actually, I was much closer to my father and probably the child least close to my mother.

"My younger brother was very sick for a number of years," she continued. "And my mother, I'm sure, was tired and irritable, and I didn't understand it at the time. But I guess I felt neglected, that she didn't spend as much time on me. She had this enormous responsibility, which I was never sympathetic about. Now as a mother and grandmother, I realize what she was going through." Barbara Bush's gradual empathy is consistent with what Ellen Baker hears from mature women in her practice: What felt like a bad mother at age fifteen can feel like a good mother—or at least an OK mother—by fifty. As a white-haired, wiser daughter, Bush was never able to express to her mom the softening of her heart. Her mother was killed in a car accident when Bush was in her early twenties, robbing her of the opportunity to re-invent the relationship as two grown women who could be pals and equals.

Elizabeth Berg's 2004 novel, *The Art of Mending*, hammers away at the importance of making our peace with our moms while we have them within reach. The troubled mother in this book, secretive and violent, weeps for days after her own mother's death, even though the two were estranged. Pressed by one of her daughters to explain this surprising breakdown over their grandmother, who was "shadowy" at best, she responds: "Now there's no chance of anything changing. Do you understand? I'm not sorry to lose her, as she was. I'm grieving for what can never be. I'm grieving for me."

With added years tagged onto the female life span, daughters in their fifties, even sixties, have the chance to surrender their anger and create change. This often means sitting down with the enemy mother and going at it: accusing, apologizing, crying, mending, and departing as friends. These confrontations can be brutal, stomach-churning showdowns. Yet, they're worth it. Because reconciling with ✻ your mother means you won't be standing over her coffin "grieving for what can never be."

Two women portrayed in the stories that follow, Ellen and Janine, have moms who are still alive, and thus they still have an opportunity to mend relations. While the bonds between these older mothers and daughters are decidedly not love affairs, the hot rage of the past has been extinguished with time.

This chapter erupts with sagas of emotional torture and physical abuse, inflicted by mothers who were wounded themselves. "Hurt people hurt other people," says John Shuford, president of the Delaware-based Conflict Resolution Services, a firm that conducts anger and forgiveness workshops nationwide. Janine endured whipping so bloody her mother skipped her child's annual check-ups at the pediatrician for fear she would be reported to a child protection agency. Ellen gorged on food because of emotional starvation. Nonetheless, these daughters—with battle scars of the body and heart—have chosen to stand by their mothers, realizing that clinging to old hatred just poisons their own ability to love, to mother, to grow. They will never swoon with the reverence Annette holds for her goddess mom. But, like Barbara Bush, they are melting as they age and beginning to feel a new, sisterly kinship with the women who fed them, clothed them, and put up with them. They are realizing what Bush saw more clearly as she approached midlife: The mothers who harm their daughters are compromised by their own traumas.

Reading the stories that follow, we learn about explosive and indifferent mothers who re-enact what was done to them in their own homes. Their daughters are fervently attempting to break the cycle of abuse and abandonment by making sure their own children are regularly fed, even overfed, with an abundance of nurturing and love.

Polly, a fifty-one-year-old Californian, never could mend her relationship with her reclusive mother, a woman who was impossible to reach. Three years ago, her mother killed herself, at the age of seventy-three. As a child, Polly recalls returning to an eerily quiet house after school. Her mother was upstairs napping, something she did every day from 1 to 5 P.M. Instead of hugging and kissing her children and grandchildren, Polly's mother would often shake their hands. She pushed her plump daughter to be fashionably thin, putting her on diets that led to Polly's lifelong fear of being overweight, even when she's not. Her lesson is how to take a barren childhood and turn it into a blessing. "I thank my mother for showing me what not to do with my own children," says Polly.

And, although Ellen Baker never gave birth to children, in the past couple of years she has been giving birth to her true self, by reaching out to her mother and regulating her erratic and dangerous eating habits. The latter is no simple feat, breaking loose from an oppressive eating disorder that endured for more than forty years.

Ellen's Story

Clothed in a paisley silk blouse and brown tailored trousers, Ellen Baker is as lithe as a woman one-third her age. "I am not clinically anorexic, but I definitely still have issues with food," says Baker, who at five-foot-four weighs only one hundred pounds. She is seated in a black leather chair in her office near the White House, flanked by books on all sorts of afflictions. One title pops out: *Caring for Ourselves: A Therapist's Guide to Personal and Professional Well-Being.* "Therapists have issues, too," she says of this book she wrote, smiling wryly. Baker cries throughout much of the interview, as we talk about her food issues, her cool mother, and her dependence on a motherly husband. Drawing from personal insights and twenty years' experience counseling women, Baker shows how elderly mothers, even the icy ones, are capable of thawing—and growing up, too.

The mother-daughter connection is immensely complex and has an impact on all areas of a daughter's life. Daughters often feel shame about the power—and the confusion therein—of that bond, which may actually feel more like bondage.

I've seen a number of adult women in my practice over the years who have felt frustrated and ashamed about still feeling stuck in their relationship with their mother. Stuck feeling young, dependent, and less than whole; stuck fighting the mother.

The hopeful news is that, as human beings, we have the potential to grow, to continue developing. Women, moving from their late forties into their fifties, not only experience developmental changes physically, involving menopause, but often emotionally as well, in their relationship with their mothers.

Many of these women, who also have their own daughters, describe becoming more able to see and experience their mothers as real people, with limits and imperfections. There is relief, and liberation, in that realization.

For many women, the battle goes way back. As children, we look to our mothers to take care of us. By the time we reach our young adult years, there is excitement about going off into the world on our own. Then, as we bumble along and hit obstacles, we start to see the truth about our mothers and feel sad or mad about what we did get or didn't get as a child. Because our mothers are human beings who were raised by human beings who were raised by human beings, they have many imperfections.

Very soon in young adulthood, the euphoria of venturing out on our own is counter-balanced with the very real bumps of being in the real world. We may start to wish that we are still protected and cared for by our idealized mother. And that's the crux of the battle: For many of us, we wish that somebody was here to take care of us, that somebody would be perfectly caring, perfectly loving, would never leave us. And of course, if you expect that from your imperfect mother, you are setting both of you up for failure. So not only are you dealing with the disappointment, but maybe you're even dealing with something else: that the person you thought was supposed to take care of you never really did. And then you get angry.

A mother is supposed to symbolize caring and ultimate protection. If we really go to an unconscious level, we start out merged, and although we have a desire to venture off and individuate, there is conflict between wanting to separate and wanting to go back to the mother.

I'm thinking of my clients, but I'm drawing from my own struggle as well. I developed an eating disorder at the age of fifteen centered around a rupture with my mother that we never spoke about. Many of us grew up in a culture where food was an expression of caring. For me, emotional nourishment was in short supply, contributing to my vulnerability for looking to food as a substitute connection with my mother.

As a high school sophomore, five-foot-four and weighing a normal one hundred fifteen pounds, I started experimenting with my diet. My mother was always on and off diets— and still is, at eighty-seven years old. At fifteen, I just assumed that dieting was part of being a woman and that being thin was necessary to being perceived as attractive. The problem was, as a fifteen-year-old, my sense of moderation or regulation was less developed than my mother's. My form of dieting was to not eat or drink anything for three days.

Of course, after three days of eating virtually nothing, I would be ravenous and then lose control, bingeing mainly on sweets and carbohydrates. I'd then swing back to abstinence, followed by the inevitable loss of control on the day I did start eating. I will forever remember the day my eating disorder took over my life. It was in late December of 1960, the Christmas holidays, and a boy from my biology class had suggested that we meet at the movies—very innocent by today's standards. The morning of the movie date, my friend Carole asked if I wanted to go coat shopping with her and her mother. I told my mother about the two invitations. She responded in a stern voice that I should go coat shopping with Carole. Meeting the boy was not something she even wanted to discuss.

This disappointment also happened to be day three of my binge-starve eating regimen. We did end up coat shopping. Back at Carole's house, after three days of starving, I proceeded, in her presence, to systematically work my way through the refrigerator, shelf by shelf. Carole's family always had lovely food in their refrigerator, and I remember eating a whole box of petits fours—and much, much more. I ate to the point of bloat and nausea. In addition to feeling physically ill, I felt emotionally mortified. The loss of control, to me and in front of my friend, was humiliating.

That winter in the northern Chicago suburbs was particularly dark, cold, and bleak. I felt that way inside as well. My confident personality and good grades both deflated. I felt depressed. I began the experience of a split life—of a public self, and a hidden one. Overtly, I behaved like the good eldest child that I was. In retrospect, I came to see that I had no trust that my mother could understand or accept the part of me that was becoming interested in boys, the sexual part of me that was separate and different from the "good girl" part of me.

To stage an open conversation about my evolving self felt too risky. I could not handle losing her approval. Her way of dealing with anything that was emotionally charged was to walk out of the room or to shut down. At this stage of her life, she exhibited classic signs of her generation and of her Germanic background; she was emotionally shut down and unexpressive. There was no talking anything out. There was minimal physical or emotional affection. I believe my obsession with dieting started because of this; in effect, it was easier to have a relationship with food than to try to have a relationship with my mother. Food was a comfort. Comfort wasn't going to come from her. Focusing on dieting provided a powerful diversion. Feeling fat from overeating and weak from undereating thoroughly diverted me from emerging sexual feelings that felt threatening to my relationship with my mother. In contemporary psychology terminology, my "dysregulated eating" became an obsession.

Food is our primal connection with our mother. Dysregulated relations with yourself, in the form of an eating disorder, reflect erratic, unsteady relations between mother and child. And overeating is often a crude attempt to self-nourish, to self-comfort. In retrospect, I can see now that the more disconnected I felt from my mother, the more I abused my own body.

The first autumn away at college, I, like many other freshman women in dorms across America, gained twenty pounds, seemingly within weeks. That fall, 1963, was explosive in other ways as well. On Friday, November 22, President Kennedy was shot. My boyfriend at the time and I also broke up that weekend. After the breakup, I returned to my dorm room and proceeded to lose control—throwing things around the room, and at the large glass window, frightening my roommate. I also swallowed a handful of aspirin as an indirect plea for help.

The dorm advisor stepped in and referred me immediately to the student health center. The recommendation from the student health center was that I was to meet weekly with a social worker to talk about my feelings and to also see a physician regularly to monitor my eating. The social worker was an older woman who was warm and kind. We are talking 1963. There was no public discussion of bulimia or anorexia at that time. I felt very deviant, and alone. With the steadying assistance of these two nurturing "good mothers," I was getting both physical and emotional support. But the obsessive roller-coaster ride of dieting and weight obsessions continued through the rest of college.

I married my husband during the fall of 1968, a few months before my twenty-third birthday. He was different from any other man I'd known, caring, warm, emotionally available. He has been someone whom I could talk to about anything. It wasn't until I'd been married for awhile that I grew more disappointed, sad, and angry with my mother's emotional limits.

We didn't have children. That choice relates, in part, to our early married years that correlated with the burgeoning women's movement of the early 1970s. The notion that a woman had the right to choose her childbearing future was a big deal. I also savored being the only recipient of the love and attention in our marriage. As the oldest of five children, I know quite well what it's like to share.

I have grown significantly since those early days of marriage, making progress in learning how to care for myself. Yet, to this day, I would say I don't have a normal relationship with food. I highly manage my intake, comparable to a diabetic. Eating in this controlled way is probably a way of assuring a sense of control, just like bingeing is a way of losing control. After feeling like I had little control with my mother, it is undeniably gratifying to have a sense of control over my own self.

As I have changed, so has my mother. The most real conversation I've ever had with my mom was just this past spring. We were in the living room of their condominium in Naples, Florida. I took a deep breath and then shared with her a very challenging, intimate problem in my marriage of thirty-seven years, which may have a non-conventional outcome. My historically non-empathetic mother responded: "Parents are usually concerned about how their children are treated. And we have always known that your husband is very good to you and cares for you. We accept him." My mother was more present with me for this hard conversation than she's ever been before. She didn't leave the room, literally or figuratively. She didn't get angry. She stayed calm and expressed a deep caring for my husband, which is ultimately a display of deep caring for me. This was the first time I remembered my mother participating in a conversation about my emotions and feelings. I had new pride and respect for her. It was apparent that she had grown.

Being able to be forthright with my mother about a sensitive personal matter feels like a long-awaited gift. When I was fifteen, we were unable to talk about sexuality. Now, with me nearing sixty, and my mother at eighty-seven, she is open to sitting down with me and accepts what I am sharing.

What I'm working on now is to let go of my need to be mothered by my husband and to become a whole self, on my own. I am growing as my mother continues to grow. It is beautiful to experience more connection with my mother as she has become more expressive of herself as a person. I can see my mother's strengths. I can let go of trying to please her at the sacrifice of myself. It took six decades, but I am gradually taking over the responsibility of being my own good mother.

The difficulty of sustaining a healthy body and mind, after stiff and cold mothering, reminds me of the famous experiments with primates conducted in the 1950s by psychologist Harry Harlow. As described in the textbook *Principles of General Psychology*, Harlow separated sixty infant monkeys from their mothers six to twelve hours after birth and gave them two "surrogate mothers," one made with a wire and wood frame, the other covered with soft fabric.

In one of the experiments, both types of substitute mothers were present in the cage, but only one was outfitted with an artificial nipple connected to formula, from which the baby could nurse. Some infants were given nourishment from the wire mother, and others were fed from the cloth mother.

Yet, even when the wire mother was the source of food, the babies spent more time clinging to the cloth surrogates.

(When the cloth monkey had the bottle, they didn't go to the wire model at all.) Primate infants, who, like humans, show a variety of emotions, clearly preferred cuddling with the cozier cloth surrogate, particularly when the pseudo-mom was covered with spongy rubber, sheathed in flesh-toned terry cloth, and lit by a bulb that radiated heat. The monkeys even cuddled with folded gauze diapers, which were used as floor covering in their cages, exhibiting an intrinsic, early need for tender touching.

"The infants clung to these pads and engaged in violent temper tantrums when the pads were removed and replaced for sanitary reasons," Harlow stated. When startled or afraid, Harlow's monkeys always ran toward the cuddly mothers and grabbed them.

Harlow's studies, conducted at the Primate Laboratory of the University of Wisconsin, have been interpreted to show that infants attach to mothers because of soothing physical contact, as well as for nourishment. And if the initial bonding is interrupted, bizarre behaviors can surface later in life. Isolate monkeys, or those taken from their mothers at birth, often clutched themselves, repeatedly rocked back and forth, and exhibited abnormal sexual responses. Once the surrogate-raised monkeys became what Harlow called "motherless mothers" themselves, their capacity for loving and caring proved to be grossly inadequate, exemplified in their failure to nurse, protect, or comfort their offspring. Some of the mothers became blatantly abusive, biting, slashing, even killing their babies.

Janine's response to her disconnected and violent mother mirrors that of Harlow's motherless monkeys. Lonely and incensed at her dearth of mother-love, Janine nearly killed herself with alcohol, extreme exercising, and years of severe bulimia. Janine feels that her dysfunction with food, her source of physical nourishment, was sparked by a misfire in her connection with her mother—supposedly her source of emotional nourishment. Despite her mother's unspeakable cruelty, Janine is supportive of her mother as she becomes increasingly frail with age. "Running from her is like running from myself," she says, understanding that to fully love herself, she must accept her mother and the abusive history that formed her.

Janine's Story ✤

Janine's mother, Elizabeth, grew up poor in the hills of West Virginia, one of six children born to a single mother who worked two jobs and was always tired and testy. Elizabeth got out, marrying at nineteen, and had two children by the time she was twenty-two. The family moved to her husband's sprawling family farm in southern coastal Georgia. When they divorced ten years later, Elizabeth got the kids and the land. Raised in a strict household where children were expected to be perfect and punishment was severe, Elizabeth, too, beat her kids as a means of discipline.

"She was not meant to be a mother. She doesn't even like little children; she thinks they are horrible," says Janine, a reedy, earthy woman who grows herbs for local health-food stores. We are walking on a pristine stretch of beach strewn with mussel shells near her home in Maine. Tousled by the salty air, Janine's gray hair falls in waves that hide her face. Having survived childhood beatings, bulimia, alcoholism, and a bad divorce that produced "one great daughter," Janine is surprisingly subdued, though not by antidepressants, as she takes on the Herculean task of "trying to get out from under my mother," a challenging work-in-progress.

My mother grew up dirt poor and her mother worked all the time; by day she was a cleaning lady, at night she waited tables. Her father was an alcoholic who was never home. There was definitely abuse in that house. When she met my father, although she wasn't overboard in love, she was left with three choices: Keep living in her dreadful home. Start college. Or marry a man from a wealthy family. So at the age of nineteen, she became a bride. Bam, my sister, was born a year later, and then I came a year after that. My first memory of my mother—I was probably three—was when I was riding my tricycle with my sister on the road leading to our farmhouse. And my mother would wave to me, go out through the gate and disappear, literally for hours. She would just take off and go exploring in the woods. She left us alone often when we were very young.

When I was eight, my mother and father split up, and we stayed on his family's 500-acre farm in Georgia. We spent most of our time with her, and my dad would sometimes fly down from New York to spend weekends with us. My memory, again, is of my mother leaving us alone, to go off and supervise the work in the fields. My sister and I would spend hours playing by ourselves outdoors. We would make forts and mud towns, and we'd play with little figures. What strikes me now is that none of my make-believe families had a mother; the mother would have been killed in some disaster.

We had a close family friend who lived down the hill from us, and years later he told me that he would come walking over to our house and find these two dirty little kids, playing alone. He couldn't believe that my mother would just leave us. But she didn't think twice about it. She would be out there with her fruit trees and soybeans. I'm telling you, this woman is not a mother—to leave a child completely by herself? Then, she started to take my older sister along with her; the two of them were close. And I would be stuck behind in this dead-silent house on this huge piece of land. I used to pray to God that a hobo would show up so I could have someone to talk to.

Another strong memory is when my grandmother came back from France and she brought me a really beautiful doll. And I sat on the back steps of our house, and I held this doll and started taking off her clothes. My mother grabbed the doll away from me, and I never saw it again. She hated dolls; she never let me have them. It was too girly. In her mind, my sister was a girl but I was a boy. As I've talked over my childhood with all these different people—therapists, friends, nuns—they always ask me if I was sexually abused. And I tell them, no, but I was gender abused. I wasn't treated like a girl. I wasn't allowed to have girly things. It made my mother really uncomfortable.

She was boyish, always dressed in jeans and denim shirts and bulky boots, and she wore her hair in a long braid tucked into a cowboy hat. Yet, she was very beautiful. Everyone always said to me, "Your mother is gorgeous." Great, but I wanted my mother to be a mother; her looks didn't get me very far.

Her family background, unschooled and rough, and her mother's impossible standards for perfection, just turned her into a very, very angry person. And I got her misplaced anger, not my sister. For some reason, she was spared. My mother would hit me with wire coat hangers and whips, depending on where I got caught doing something wrong. Like, if I was at the barn, she would hit me with a horse whip. If I was in the house, she'd beat me with a coat hanger. I remember thinking by the age of nine, "I'm not that bad. Why does my mother beat me? This is not fair." The beating was so bad one time she canceled my pediatric check-up so the doctor wouldn't see my welts.

I definitely acted out. I got kicked out of two nursery schools in one year because I was so out of control. I beat up kids. I threw blocks at kids. I wasn't acting out because I was a bad child. I was acting out what was being done to me. My father caught my mother beating me once. It was so bad he slapped her and said, "Don't you ever hit her again." But it didn't do any good once he was gone.

I never told my mother to stop hitting me. I was terrified of her. She didn't think she was doing anything wrong. I got used to her violent outbursts. She would get wildly angry, over little things. I remember once there were some turkeys making noise outside and she told our farmhand Ray to go outside immediately and shoot all of them. So Ray goes outside and shoots a dozen turkeys. One morning she wakes up and looks out the window and decides our old oak tree is blocking her view. She grabs a chain saw, stomps outside, and just cuts it up, like's she's cutting its head off and murdering it.

As a teenage girl going through the typical swings of adolescence, I did think, "Wouldn't it be nice to have a mother *to talk to?" But I never had my mother. She was missing, and when she was there, she was either mad at me or about to go out the door to tend to the crops or to her animals. At night, she never had dinner with us. I would throw something together for myself, and my mother would go lie on her bed in a dark room with a bottle of wine and listen to Bob Dylan. My sister and my mother were like a little team against me. They would make up these names for me. Like, they called me Pizza Nose. They told me my body looked like a fire hydrant.*

Nothing stings and shapes a daughter's self-image like a mother's comments on her appearance. Artist Georgia O'Keeffe, striking and sensual even as a very old woman, was, as a young girl, "shut in a back room when company called; her mother judged her too ugly to be seen by visitors," writes biographer Benita Eisler in *O'Keeffe & Stieglitz*, her book about O'Keeffe and her on/off husband, photographer Alfred Stieglitz. This daughter, whose mother was ashamed of her homeliness, went on to paint majestic poetry into cattle skulls and landscapes. Despite her mother's failure to notice, or cultivate, her daughter's inner radiance, O'Keeffe blossomed as an artist famous for her feminine shapes and timeless sexuality. A series of nudes of O'Keeffe, shot by Stieglitz, reveals a gorgeous woman who dwells with unabashed pride in her body. Emotionally and physically, Janine is still trying to heal from her mother's digs.

Because of the verbal assaults on my appearance, it is very hard for me to feel comfortable and sexually open, after the way my mother handled my femininity. I have really worked on self-esteem and sexual expression during years and years of therapy and after the failure of my marriage to an uncommunicative man. My mother just became this huge presence that has pervaded my whole life. There's so much stuff with me that's still tied to her; our farm, money issues. She is my daughter's grandmother. As I've grown, I have come to see there are things that my mother gave me that represent the best part of my childhood and remain a central and wonderful part of who I am. She gave me my love for animals, my love of flowers and plants. We always had a garden with beautiful fruit trees. She let us have any kind of animal we wanted. I used to think my mom was part cowgirl and part Indian; she was happiest when she ran wild in the outdoors.

But she also gave me a tendency to self-destroy.

By freshman year in college, I knew I was an alcoholic. I'd drink wine at night, just like she did, and I'd barely be able to get up. Then around 11 A.M., I'd start drinking Bloody Marys. My obsession with diet and weight began around this time. I was an excessive athlete who ran eight miles a day. And then I became insane with bulimia for the next ten years or so. It was all about my mother. My bulimia was about filling up on the mother, then throwing up the mother. It was so awful. I kept thinking, "I'm going to die." I wanted my mother to die. But then I saw that if she died I'd still have all of this stuff inside of me.

We talk now, but not about what happened and not about deep issues. I have simply made the choice to be a good daughter and to be there if she needs me as she gets old. She is lonely on that farm, and ironically I visit her more than my sister does. My mother has become my friend. But she is not a mother. She is more like this interesting character in my life. All this stuff I carry around with me from my childhood is mine now. It really doesn't have anything to do with her. She's in her late seventies and on her own trip now. Lately, she's been exploring all kinds of New Age practices. She is drawn to Native American spirituality. I really think this new involvement is my mother's attempt to heal herself. This is her journey, and I wish her well. My journey is to learn how to enjoy her but not let her overpower me. My big breakthrough with my mother was when I stopped expecting her to fulfill me in any way and just accepted her for the selfish free spirit that she is.

On her seventy-fifth birthday I gave her the most amazing gift, this large Hopi Indian bowl. For my fiftieth birthday I visited her on the farm, and she said to me, "My present to you is that you're here." She does not give presents. I should know that by now. I accept that the two of us are a real mismatch. She's not emotionally generous, and I'm a giver. When I expect her to be different, what I get in return is frustration and emptiness. So I don't expect her to change anymore.

I love my mother. I forgive my mother. I honestly think she was acting out what was acted out on her. I don't blame my mother. She was a very wounded woman who just cracked from the circumstances of her life. She was punished by her mother for not being perfect. She married someone she wasn't in love with. And I think her anger and violence spun out of her feeling trapped and cornered by her own life.

I chose to learn from her horrific mistakes; my mothering style is loving and nurturing. Now that I understand the limits of who she is, I'm no longer terrified of anything she can do to me. Part of her behavior is laughable. You know, suddenly she's enlightened in the New Age. The other day I was complaining about my body and she said, "Oh Janine. You should love your body." And I just felt like throwing up. She says this like it's a new idea she has discovered, like I can switch instantly from hating my body to loving my body, after all she's put me through. As I said, I don't want her to die. I want this ghost inside of me to die. I want this big thing that's the old, bad mother inside of me to die, and something else to be born. That's my job, to figure out how I can have my own life and come out from under her.

There are a lot of things people think I need to say to my mother. But I don't feel like I need to have another conversation about the past with my mother. I don't think my mother thinks she did anything wrong, and I don't need to drag her through it. In her own way, she feels guilty. I know that. There definitely has been a shift in our relationship. Recently I was down at the farm and when I was leaving she asked me to stay for the rest of the day. I guess she feels some of the loneliness now that I felt as a child. I looked at my watch and said, "Mother, I can stay for about ten more minutes, then I need to go." We talked for a while and then I hugged her goodbye. She started to cry in my arms. Now, this is something I've not seen before. It is very rare to see her weepy and needy. And it is rare for me to be the tough one.

But I am the stronger one now. I'm re-birthing in middle age, and she's entering old age. And because I am a caring person, I can't just abandon her now. But it is a fine line: How do I retain my own self and also stand by my mother? You know, there are many kinds of feelings that I'm having *today. She was extremely tough on me, for a long time, a long time ago. I was extremely sick for a really long time, very sick for more than a decade. I was in therapy for sixteen years. I could be very, very angry at her. But I don't drink anymore. I'm at a good weight. I have a trusting new relationship with a wonderful man. So in many ways, what my mother did to me is really ancient history. I'm really OK.*

Janine's weight is now normal. She is increasingly confident in her sexuality. And she is willing to forgive her mother for unforgivable acts. These milestones, despite the terror of her childhood, are the result of the compassion that comes with age. At one point, Janine silently wished for her mother's death; now, she is more concerned with getting on with her own life. Some daughters with a similar death wish are unable to keep a lid on it. A friend from my old Chicago neighborhood hurt so badly from her mother's hands and cruel barbs that she said, "I wish it were you" the day the family buried her seventy-one-year-old father.

A mother's words and actions can sting a daughter like nothing else. But a daughter can do an effective job of zinging her mother, too. And the quintessential agony for a mom must come from hearing her daughter say, "I wish you were dead." In Amy Tan's *The Bonesetter's Daughter*, Ruth can't contain her feelings toward her cloying Chinese mother, LuLing, a woman who keeps threatening to kill herself in order to rile her daughter. Like Janine and Ellen, Ruth's stomach twists with emotions about a mother she can't escape, as they cohabitate in a bungalow so cramped it feels like a "doll house." As Tan describes it: "The combined living room, eating area, and efficiency kitchen afforded no place to hide. Ruth's only refuge was the bathroom, and perhaps for this reason she developed numerous stomach ailments."

Unwound by lack of privacy and a barrage of criticism, Ruth vents her fury in her diary, which she knows her mother always reads: "I hate her! She's the worst mother a person could have. She doesn't love me. She doesn't listen to me. She doesn't understand anything about me. All she does is pick on me, get mad, and make me feel worse.

"You talk about killing yourself, so why don't you ever do it? I wish you would. Just do it, do it, do it. Go ahead, kill yourself!"

Just as Ruth anticipated, her mother reads the diary. As Ruth doesn't anticipate, however, her mother does what she encouraged her to do. LuLing jumps out a window and is whisked by ambulance to the emergency room, where she lies with a broken shoulder, a cracked rib, and a concussion. As she heals over a span of weeks, LuLing is eerily silent about her daughter's death wish for her. "She acted not angry but sad and defeated," writes Tan. "And each day, several times a day, Ruth wanted to tell her mother that she was sorry, that she was an evil girl, that everything was her fault. But to do so would be to acknowledge what her mother obviously wanted to pretend never existed, those words Ruth had written. For weeks, they walked on tiptoe, careful not to step on the broken pieces."

The Bonesetter's Daughter chronicles Ruth's search for "the evaporating past" of her mother's family, an excavation of tumult and mystery that draws this daughter closer to her mother, as she finds "what they share in their bones through heredity, history, and inexpressible qualities of love." The daughter in Amy Tan's book and the ones on these pages discover that what they share in their bones with their mothers can solidify the bond and soften anger. When we discover that our mothers had mothers who caused them their own stomachaches, we can start owning their pain too and stop feeling like their victims. By examining our mothers' history, it is easier to go forward with fresh hope and empathy. Janine was whipped and so was her mother. This doesn't make it right, but it makes a bad mother easier to understand.

Polly's Story

Polly never had the opportunity to dig to the root of her mother's pain, although she and her brothers assumed their mother was hurting deeply. "Deep conversations were not what my mother was about," explains Polly. "So I don't know exactly what happened in her own childhood." And now there's no chance to find out. In February of 2002, her mother took a handful of pills, stuck a bag over her head, and died in her sleep. Sitting in a green director's chair in her backyard in northern California, Polly tells me she "wished I had pushed my mother to talk." Mostly, however, she feels relief that her mother, dark and detached, is no longer there. She is not saddled with guilt. Her mature take on the way her mother lived and died is that "it's not about me; it was about her own pain."

Amidst flowering magnolias and pear trees, Polly pauses often to gather her thoughts. She wears no makeup, and her straight brown hair hangs like that of Mary Travers of the singing group Peter, Paul, and Mary. She talks about her mother in a solemn voice that doesn't once crack. The unusual payoff for having a mother who rarely embraced her is that she has raised two grown sons who know, through her tender touch, the depth of her love: "Whatever she did with me, I did the opposite," she says. Here is more from Polly.

My mother was always very withdrawn. In later years, she would never even go out anywhere. She rarely even left the house. The first three years of my life we had a full-time nanny, so she didn't even take care of me as a baby. I have no memory of her holding me or being warm. She was uncomfortable about showing emotion or love. The nanny left when I was three; then my mother did have to take care of me. And of course she did. But she wasn't involved in the physical or emotional ways that mothers are supposed to be involved. I spent a lot of time alone, in a smoky house. She chain-smoked Tareytons.

By the time I was ready for high school, I was sent away to boarding school. My brothers had been sent away for high school also. She just didn't want to deal with us. This is a woman who had children not because of some maternal urge, but because that was the thing to do. I really think she realized that she wasn't a good mom, and that probably made her more frustrated.

My mom took a nap every day for as long as I remember, from one in the afternoon until five. Can you imagine doing that? She'd have lunch, go upstairs, and take a nap. Then she'd get up and fix dinner, have a couple of drinks, bourbon. For a while, as a kid, I thought that was normal. I had another friend down the street and her mom was the same as mine: nap, make dinner, drink, fall back asleep. So for a while I thought, "This is the way moms are."

As a child, I was very quiet and withdrawn, too. I learned from my mother that you don't express your emotions. It's still hard for me to do, at the age of fifty. After years of therapy, I'm getting better at it. But it sure doesn't come easy for me. I know as a child you need love and comfort, and where was I was getting that? To tell you the truth, it was through food. I've always had eating issues. I just kind of filled myself up with food instead of getting the love I needed. Starting in third grade, I was one of the heavier girls. When I was in seventh grade, my mom put me on a diet, and she did that again in the ninth grade. She told me I was fat and that made me eat more, but it also made me exercise madly. My brother remembers that I would swim laps and laps and laps in the pool.

I did not talk about my loneliness or sadness with my dad. He was like most dads of that time. He went to work, came home. And when he was at home, he liked to relax; they would have their cocktails and watch the news and play backgammon. During the four years of boarding school, I came home for every vacation. Each time, before I went back to school, I would cry that I didn't want to return. I loved my father, and I wanted to stay home. I hated boarding school.

I would have expected some comfort from my mother since she rarely saw me. Maybe, since she saw I was miserable, I could transfer to a school closer to home. This never happened; she just didn't have it in her to deal with having her children around. You know, she was motherly in some ways, such as giving nice presents. She remembered all of our birthdays. But I never heard her say "I love you" to me or to my children. I remember when we were visiting my parents with our sons. One of my boys—he was six at the time—he went to give his grandmother a hug, and she put out her hand for him to shake instead.

I went to college in California, and fairly early on, I met Paul, the man who would become my husband. We starting living together in college, and married in 1978, when I was only twenty-four. I was young when I married because I was definitely looking for the family connection that I didn't have. Frankly, I was very insecure and still struggling with food. My weight was up and down. I still have eating issues. I still struggle with it. I still feel heavy even when I'm not.

Physical appearance was very important to my mother, obviously. When I was born, I was cross-eyed, my ears stuck out, I was knock-kneed and pigeon-toed. I had surgery to correct everything. You know, she thought a daughter was a reflection of her, and she wanted me to be slim and presentable. Throughout my life, I always felt like I needed to lose weight.

My husband has been a great comfort throughout all of this. He loves to hold hands. He is naturally warm and very physical. He doesn't criticize my looks. We have a normal and loving relationship. When we had kids, that's when I really realized how weird my mother was. I just loved my children from day one. I couldn't stop touching them. When we would visit my parents with our kids, my mother would tell me to put them in a crib and if they cry, so what? I told her that I just couldn't do that. And she would look at me and say, "Well, that's what I did." That's when I started figuring out that not everyone was like her. She always told me that I spoiled my kids, held them too much. Still, she's my mother, right? And I did want to spend time with her and have my children know their grandmother. But she was basically a recluse. She wouldn't take airplanes and did not want to endure the long drive from Pasadena to see us in northern California. If I brought it up to her, she would tell me that it was my problem, not hers. She never admitted she had any problems whatsoever.

I keep asking myself, "How do I keep from turning into her?" Actually, I think I'm a really good mom, and the reason I am is because of her: I saw what not to do. In that sense, I'm very grateful to her. I tell my boys all the time that I love them. I never in my whole life had a heart-to-heart talk with my mother. I would have liked to talk to her about what went wrong in her own life to make her this way.

My brothers and I would always try to figure out what happened to her, why she was the way she was. We knew that her parents died when she was very young, and that she was raised by her brother and sister, who were twenty and twenty-two years older than her. I would have loved to know my mother, but she was not capable of a conversation that would be honest or deep. I learned through many years of therapy that it wasn't my fault. It wasn't my fault that instead of wanting to pick us up after school, she hired someone to drive carpool. It wasn't my fault that when I came home at 4 P.M., she'd rather take a nap than greet me. It wasn't my fault that she was not willing to dig deeper in our relationship. I came to accept that she just didn't have the skills to be a mother because she wasn't mothered herself.

Although I have come a long way, it is still hard for me to open up to people. I don't like parties. I am really shy and quiet. Yet, I am not a depressed person. I have a lot of love in my own home, and a lot to be happy about. Over the last few years, when I did see my mother, it was clear that she was getting increasingly depressed. I saw her for the last time Thanksgiving of 2001. It was the usual Thanksgiving. My brothers were there with their families. We all went out to dinner, my parents, their three children and five grand-children. My mother had quit smoking, but she did have emphysema, although it wasn't that bad. My feeling that day was that here was a woman who obviously wanted to die, and the emphysema wasn't killing her fast enough.

On a Friday three months later, my father called, and my husband answered the phone. I could tell by the look on his face that something very bad had happened. He said, "Your mom died," and I just burst out crying. He told me that it looked like a suicide. She took a bunch of sleeping pills, put a plastic bag over her head, and suffocated in her sleep. My father found her in the late afternoon. I flew to their home right away.

This was definitely her way out—of not having to hon-estly deal with any family or relationships ever again. Her suicide was orchestrated perfectly. She had read a book on suicide; the coroner even knew the name of the book—he could tell by her death. My immediate feeling was profound sadness. Then I got really mad at her when I saw her suicide note a couple of weeks later. The letter was solely directed at my dad.

She told him how much she loved him. And at the end of this nice letter to him, she listed day-to-day things he needed to handle. You know, RSVP to this wedding and buy them a present. Cancel these doctor's appointments. But she didn't say one word about her kids, nothing. But soon after feeling this anger, I really did start to feel relief. She had been depressed for so long. I wasn't shocked that my mother took her own life, because she had always been self-absorbed.

She was cremated, and we went on my father's boat out to a beautiful spot by Catalina Island and sprinkled her ashes. This was a boat she had never even seen because she didn't like to leave her zip code. In the last years of her life, the only place she would go was to the market. And about once a month, she would go to the country club and have lunch, and that was about it, in terms of leaving the house.

Even though her death was awful, I have no guilt. I had really come to terms with her before she died. I had realized that who she was, and the nature of our relationship, wasn't my fault. So her death isn't haunting me, even though it was grisly, because it was her choice, and it was a peaceful death. She went to sleep, and she didn't suffer. She suffered a lot during her life. One year to the day after my mother's death, my father died from complications of surgery to remove a brain tumor.

I loved my father and he knew that, even though we didn't talk about it a lot. And he was a wonderful grandfather to my children. I guess my regret with my mother is that I wished I had tried to talk to her more. As I'm telling you this, I do see that I miss her at times. She was, after all, my mother. Sometimes I wish I could talk to her about something; not necessarily a deep conversation, but just get a recipe or something like that. But now I'm not mad at her. I am grateful because she made me a good mother.

Polly's disappearing mother is reminiscent of the self-absorbed woman who raised author Ann Roiphe. In her book *Fruitful: A Real Mother in the Modern World*, Roiphe captures the sorrow of a daughter whose mother would soak for hours in the bathtub, sipping scotch, too lost in herself to pay attention to her family. That was the job of servants. Here she describes her mother's indifference:

> She was there, but I couldn't reach her.
>
> When I was sick for long periods throughout the year with the earaches that would take me in those pre-antibiotic days, my mother would not come into my room. The governess would sit by my bed, solid, functional, unwanted by me, fussing with steam kettles, hot-water bottles, soft-boiled eggs. I would wait for a glimpse of my mother, a flash of a gold bracelet, a black hat with a net veil, pausing at the door. She was afraid of illness and would enter the room only when the fever was gone.

I am thinking of Janine and Polly, the products of tough mothers who are in turn the products of tough mothers, and how they are breaking the cycle with their own kids. And I know my own mother's tragic past played out in my childhood. I think of the stories in this book and the mothers of many of my girlfriends and am reminded again of how different their lives were from their daughters' lives.

Polly's mother obviously suffered from clinical depression, but there was often a more subtle malaise that was common among the housewives of the 1950s and 1960s, women afflicted with what Betty Friedan called "the trapped housewife syndrome." The mothers we had gripes about growing up under generally didn't have avenues for self-fulfillment or personal growth. In their pre-feminist roles, they had no adventurous jobs to go to after the kids went off to school. Like my mother, they often sat alone with their knitting and crossword puzzles and cigarettes at their kitchen tables. They cooked and they cleaned and they made PTA phone calls, while their husbands got to flex their ambitions and intellects in professional pursuits.

As Friedan writes in her book that helped launch the modern feminist movement, *The Feminine Mystique:* "The tragedy of marriage is not that it fails to assure woman the promised happiness—there is no such thing as assurance in regard to happiness—but that it mutilates her; it dooms her to repetition and routine . . . Real activities, real work, are the prerogative of her man; she has mere things to occupy her, which are sometimes tiring, but never satisfying."

Indeed, my mother became a nicer, more ebullient woman when she started working outside of the home. That vision of her, purposefully striding down Michigan Avenue with the wind whipping her silk scarf, is what I hold onto, and not the bad stuff. I feel like Janine—I turned out OK, and I don't blame her for anything. She did what she could, given her circumstances. There's no time left for sour memories. I don't have ten to twenty years remaining with my mother. All I have is this moment now.

I am a graying daughter at age fifty, and she is my sick mother at age eighty-five. Both of us have friends who have died or are dying from cancer or heart disease. We are two vulnerable women living on borrowed time with open eyes about all that has gone between us. There are no more masks or charades, no more stubbornly holding onto our acts—me the rebellious teenager, she the unflinching stoic. I no longer want to fight her; she no longer wants to pretend she's stronger than everyone else. An old lady with one leg needs a lot of love, and my mother is not ashamed to ask for it. There is no more fear of saying something wrong or hurting the other person; we've already done enough of that. Now we are free to simply be, unclouded by past skirmishes. As time runs out, our focus must be on bringing each other pleasure, today.

Growing up, I wasn't too skinny or too fat, but I knew how to make my mother mad at meals. And that was to pick at my food, pushing the peas to one side, taking a couple of meager bites of chicken. My sister and brother and I have heard a thousand times how she scavenged in garbage cans for food while she was dodging Nazis in France during the German occupation; and so nothing could go to waste in our house. After years of going hungry, she wanted to make sure her children's tummies were filled. We were a family that couldn't have dessert, or even leave the table, before our plates were clean. I hear my mother in me when I repeat her mantra at the table with my boys, "Eat, eat, eat—or you won't get your cookies."

I still get stomachaches when I'm with my mother, but they're not from anger. My stomach is ripped with sadness because she is fading. It is hard for her to swallow now, or to feed herself, and she is finicky about food. When I visit, I bring the treats she loves the most: smoked salmon, runny cheeses, fresh figs, and Hershey bars. And I force her to eat, just as she once forced me to eat, putting small morsels directly into her mouth. Then I warn her: If she doesn't eat everything on her plate, she won't get any chocolate.

When our hard mothers become soft, we soften too. We are their daughters, after all; they are in our bones. I'm done with rage. I held onto anger about my mother's failure to be what I considered to be "normal" for a long, long time—for thirty-five years, from adolescence into my mid-forties. I kept waiting for her to become a mother like my friend Rose seemed to have, someone who would buy me bikini underwear, make nail appointments for us together, ask me for details about my fears, my dreams, my work. None of this happened. In the several years I roamed the world as a feature writer for UPI, or United Press International, my mother used to tell people I worked for UPS, or United Parcel Service. This was a natural slip for a foreigner who spoke English as a second language. Yet, the mistake was revealing of her nature: She knew I was a journalist and not a dispatcher of mail, but she was oblivious to the details of my career, or the subtleties of me, in general. She was concerned only with the big picture—that I was healthy and productive.

Hungering for closer communication, I often came away famished, like this description by Dr. Christiane Northrup in her book *Mother-Daughter Wisdom:*

> She keeps going back to the well of maternal attention to try to slake her thirst for unconditional recognition and approval, because for generations her cells have been programmed to do this. Though she sometimes gets a few sips of her mother's approval, there is never enough to truly fill her up and the price is very high. She is being called upon to bear the brunt of her mother's unhappiness and lack of fulfillment. At the very time when she

needs most her mother's support to move ahead in her own life, her mother is calling her back.

This wisdom from Northrup, a mother of two daughters, reminds me of the many times my mother has broken my heart. I know I've broken her heart too, leaving home and never returning, to northern California for college, to write for the *Dallas Times Herald*, then for the UPI Bureau in Washington, D.C., a part of the country where I still live. Recently she looked me right in the eye and said, "You deserted me," and it was like a knife into that vulnerable stomach of mine.

When I was small, I used to pray that she would burst out of her armor and turn into Donna Reed: cheery, fawning, blonde. Alas, my brunette mom could never be anything other than who she is, a creature of her history. Motherless early, how could she become classically maternal? She could not. This is the mother I got, and it's an irrevocable deal. Letting go comes a lot easier when you are old enough to comprehend that mothers become the mothers they are because of the mothers they had, or did not have. This release could not have happened when I was twenty-five or thirty-five or even forty, when I was still hankering for something that I was never going to get—all-out adoration and lots of stroking. At fifty, I get who she is and who I am, and I see that there are clear limits. I've grown to love her authenticity.

I ask myself today if my gypsy roving was necessary to grow away from my mother, and I cannot answer that question definitively. I do know that no matter how far I have traveled, my mother has moved in with me. From her kitchen in Chicago she dominates me in my kitchen in

Maryland. My mother is with me, in me, *is me*, when I cook, feed, kiss, yell, clean, and collapse into bed at 9 P.M. I also understand that a mother doesn't have to be a Holocaust survivor to feel overwhelmed and upset a lot of the time. Even the nicest storybook mothers get hissy.

"I am angry nearly every day of my life," admits Mrs. March, or Marmee, in Louisa May Alcott's *Little Women,* the timeless story of female passages told through the lives of four sisters living in Concord, Massachusetts, during the Civil War era. Marmee, the angelic mother of Meg, Jo, Beth, and Amy, seems like the last person to be harboring rage. Throughout the book she is patient, docile, compassionate, and self-sacrificing. Marmee blows her perfect cover when she reveals her anger to Jo, who also struggles with a quick temper. Jo is left wondering if she, too, will turn out to be a mother who is serene on the surface but seething within.

Feminist critics have attributed Marmee's self-professed anger to the oppression of women during the nineteenth century. But I bet that, if the truth be told, most liberated mamas today are angry, for at least a flash, once a day. I have become less judgmental of my mother's stony expressions and violent explosions during the weeks and years I have spent scheduling, shuttling, balancing, and losing it. I forgive her as I become her. That said, there *are* malevolent episodes with my mother that I replay and cannot forgive. I'm sure you can conjure up some nasty scenes with your own mom that make your stomach feel as if you'd been whammed with a baseball bat. It doesn't have to be punishment as brutal as that notoriously inflicted on Christina Crawford. In her memoir, *Mommie Dearest*, she describes how her tyrant mother, actress Joan Crawford, chopped off her hair, banged her head on the floor, beat her with a hanger, and attempted to choke her. Christina has every right to be very mad, for a very long time. Yet, far more subtle injuries can feel like torture.

Here is one of my mother's meanest moments, which still makes me wince more than thirty years later.

In the summer of 1973, I was a counselor at a day camp in Boulder, Colorado. One day my mother phoned to say that she and my father were moving to a condominium in Chicago from the suburban house I had lived in since the day I was born. It was the middle of July, and the Colorado mountains were ablaze with purple wildflowers. This was the blissful summer I fell in love with a fellow counselor and Richard Nixon resigned. Sidetracked by nature, hormones, and political turmoil, I wasn't focused on what might happen to the accumulated treasures in my bedroom where I had slept nearly every night of my life. I wasn't thinking about the fate of my wicker shelves, laden with troll dolls and animal miniatures. I was hiking with campers and my boyfriend, not wondering what a mother who was selling her house would do with her daughter's childhood clothes, framed posters, Teddy Bears, books. I didn't even ask.

When August came and camp was over, my father picked me up at the airport and took me to our new apartment on the shore of Lake Michigan, where there was one bedroom to be shared by three grown children who would now have to alternate their visits from college. I put my bags on one of the twin beds, looked around this room, with its red geometric slashes on the white walls and red shiny furniture, and shuddered. It was too clean, too modern, and there was nothing familiar in it, no clutter from two decades of raising children.

"Mom, where's my stuff?" I screamed, digging through closets and drawers.

"I sold it," she said calmly, standing in the doorway. To this day, my heart lurches as I recall those words. Trinkets and memorabilia, picked up on trips or received as gifts from people I loved, were tagged and sold to strangers looking for bargains. A woman who fled Europe with nothing but a handful of family pictures doesn't attach sentimental value to material goods. With her children away at college and eager to downsize, my mother packed up our house and sold everything in it, without a backward glance. It didn't occur to her to ask her children if they wanted to first sort out our favorite things. Later, as I read to my own children in bed at night, I longed to share my copy of *Black Beauty* with them, so I could show them the passages I underlined as a child. But it was swooped up at a sale on a front lawn in Oak Park, Illinois, along with the red cowboy boots I wore in kindergarten, my Patty Playpal, and my Woodstock posters.

The vision of that house sale is devastating, even though I wasn't there—particularly when I picture the girl who got my purple Twiggy skirt and the short white boots that I could have passed on to a granddaughter someday for a retro Halloween costume. I do not forgive my mother for dismantling eighteen years of *my life* so that *her life* would be less encumbered. I continue to ask her, "What were you thinking, Mom?" at odd times, when I remember a certain lost treasure, and she shrugs and answers, "What do you need it for?" I am a mother who knows that need is not the reason you keep old things. You keep relics of the past so that you can touch them and talk about events that led you to them that piece together who you are.

My reaction to a mother who got rid of my possessions without my permission is that I am a mother who gets rid of nothing. I have every baby tooth from every child, every poem and short story they have written, one hundred twenty-six Power Ranger figurines, every stuffed animal they chewed on and cuddled. When my boys become men, they may choose to toss everything out: It's not a decision that's mine to make. My husband is not thrilled that his wife is a compulsive pack rat with boxes stacked high in our attic and barn. Yet because of my mother, I can be no other way.

I talk about the difference between forgiving and forgetting a lot with my friends, when it comes to deeds done by our mothers. One memorable example is Lynn, who has finally begun to forget the raw agony she felt a decade ago when her mother killed her cat, Cocoa, a pet Lynn had had for eight years. Although it was an accident, Lynn says it was the culmination of "a chain of mishaps and disappointments" that she had been noticing more and more as she became an adult and mother.

Lynn's Story

At the age of forty-one, Lynn recently gave birth to her third child. Yet, she worries about his grandmother's visits because she thinks her mom "can be dangerous" around babies. With unabated bitterness, she tells of one incident with her firstborn that occurred the same weekend her cat died. Lynn went to the grocery story and left her mom alone with her toddler for one hour. When she returned, he was yowling, scared and bruised after falling down the stairs. It turned out that her mother knowingly did not latch the gate at the top of the landing when putting him down for his nap. "It was too much trouble to fiddle with the latch in order to properly lock the gate," says Lynn. So, instead her mother put the gate into what appeared to be a closed position, and Lynn's son wandered out of bed, pushed against the gate, and tumbled down the steps.

My mother is so self-focused that she doesn't pay attention to what's going on around her. This is why my baby fell down the stairs, and why Cocoa died. My mother was visiting us for a week in April of 1995. We had eaten breakfast and were getting ready for the day. My mom had been sleeping on a hideaway bed, and when she folded up the bed, she folded my cat up in it. Cocoa had been curled up sleeping underneath the blanket.

It was horrible. At 11:00 P.M. when my mom got into bed, she felt something wet against her leg. Yes, it was the dead cat. This is a pet I'd had since grad school, and I loved this cat so much. I'm not sure I have fully forgiven my mother even now. For the longest time, I couldn't even look her in the face. Thinking about Cocoa and how she died, I would cry and wonder: "How could she have done this? How careless could she be?"

When I found out about Cocoa, even though it was late at night, I ran out of the house, screaming. I was so upset and angry. I just lay there on the ground crying. It was like a culmination of everything I had been feeling about how self-centered she is. My husband said to me at the time that I had a choice: I could go back into the house and tell my mom that I understood that accidents happen and that she didn't do it on purpose. Or I could choose to end my relationship with my mother right now by telling her how I really felt. I knew that I just couldn't and wouldn't do anything that would permanently sever our relationship, as tenuous as it was. She's my mother, and I wanted to always have my mother in my life.

And so, with gritted teeth, I went to her and said: "Mom, I understand. Accidents happen. It's OK." I said all of this even though at that moment I did not understand how she could have possibly managed to kill my cat, and I still do not understand it. I think what upset me the most, other than Cocoa being dead, was that she never really did apologize in a full and heartfelt way. Maybe this would have been easier for me to get over if she would have come back to me, and said: "I'm so sorry, honey. I know how much you loved your cat. I'm so, so sorry." But there was none of that. Not even once.

Losing Cocoa made me remember a lot of important ways my mother has not been there for me, although she did have a tough life, raising four kids on not a lot of money. My father was very sickly, constantly in and out of the hospital, so she worked two jobs just to keep us afloat. I grew up admiring her for her strength. But she was also a woman who at times loved me from a distance, in ways I still find confusing and disappointing.

Let me jump back to the day I was born. I arrived a month prematurely, and we both almost died during childbirth. I ended up having to stay in the hospital for about one week after my mother was released. My father visited me in the hospital every day. My mother has told me that after she was released, she didn't once visit me in the hospital. She tells me now that she just couldn't handle it; I was just about four pounds and it was hard for her to see me struggling. And she tells me this without remorse. Now that I have my own children whom I am so deeply attached to I am shocked that a mother wouldn't want to stay with her premature infant every single second of every single day that baby is in the hospital.

But that's my mother. And when I think of how our relationship has been most of my life, I wonder if our distance emotionally may have something to do with her being subconsciously mad at me that my birth nearly made her lose her life. It was my father who brought me home from the hospital. That image of coming home in his arms and not hers is really reflective of the type of arms-length dynamic we continue to have.

It's now more than four decades later, but I would describe my overall feeling for my mother as one of love, but tinged with disappointment.

In high school I was on the swim team, which I loved, and practice was right after school. I would be done around six at night, and my mom would usually pick me up. I would have a wet head, and my mom pretty much gave me so much crap about running around with a wet head, and swimming instead of helping out with household chores, that I quit the swim team and stopped doing something I loved.

I still feel sad and sometimes angry about my mother. Something big was missing from what I got from her growing up. I remember my friends having these cozy chats with their moms during adolescence. My mother never told me about the facts of life. Nothing about my period. I came home one day and said, "Hey, Mom, guess what I learned today?" and she had very little to say about it. I have not forgotten that horrible day that my mother killed my cat and how that opened up all sorts of other pain about the past. Now, she's in physical decline, with heart and back problems, and I try to be there for her whenever she calls. She doesn't live in the same state as I do, and with three small children, it's difficult to physically be there for her. But I try to be helpful. Yet, when I need someone to take care of me, I look more toward my husband or to my older sister.

Recently I had major surgery, and my mother did not come to the hospital, nor did she offer to help at home during the weeks of my recovery. In fact, she said that she knew she'd be more help by not coming to stay with us than by being here. I felt so sad at the time that she was "copping out" of coming, but I guess it was probably the truth. I am envious of women who have the kind of mother who wouldn't think of being anywhere else but by the side of her ailing daughter. I also wish that I had wanted nothing more than to have my mother by my side. But what can I expect? When I was a newborn, even though I didn't know it, my mother was not by my hospital bed either. As for our ongoing relationship, I just keep letting go of her behavior that hurts me. Time really does have a way of dulling our feelings and fading bad memories. I don't forget the anger. I don't think I will ever forgive her for Cocoa. But she's my mother. I love her even though she makes mistakes. At least we have a relationship and I wouldn't give it up for the world. I'm sure she loves me more than I'll ever know, just as I do her.

I am struck by Lynn's last line, about a mother who may love her more than she'll ever know. And I am wondering if my own mother will ever know the depth of my love for her.

In March of 1986, two weeks after my father died, my mother summoned her children to their apartment and assigned us to clear out his clothes and other visible signs of her mate of thirty-four years. Some grieving widows go to the other extreme, leaving their husbands' closets as they were the day they died, never laundering their shirts, bathrobes, or even the boxers they last wore. My mom's way of dealing with sudden widowhood at the age of sixty-five was to immediately remove everything, from suits to socks to toiletries. She believed in the "out of sight, out of mind" adage. As we loaded my dad's ties and sweaters and shoes into boxes, I wondered how my mother felt when she was packing up our bedrooms years ago. Maybe she was teary, pausing to sniff well-worn items for traces of our scents, just as we were doing. Maybe she quickly cleared out our bedrooms to protect herself from the despair and loneliness of being surrounded by things that belonged to beloved children who weren't there anymore.

I am preparing for the sadness of being surrounded by things that belonged to my mother, whom I loved, then hated for a while—and ended up loving so much that the loss will give me the worst stomachaches I've ever had.

chapter five

GROWING OLD TOGETHER

*No mother is the Great Goddess who is always
good. Each of us is just an ordinary woman who
tries to be as good as she can be.*

—PSYCHOLOGIST FLORENCE WIEDEMANN

A T THE AGE OF SIXTY-NINE, Betsy is the spunky director of operations at a social service agency in New Jer-
sey. Wearing a hot pink cotton sweater, she sits at a large oak
desk overflowing with papers and files. Her phone rings, and
the caller is her ninety-six-year-old mother. Betsy responds
in a series of clipped sentences: "Yes, mom. I know, mom.
Yes, mom. Don't worry, mom. Goodbye, mom." She slams
down the phone and laughs loudly.

"I'm gonna kill her! She has to control everything. Always. Everything." This time it's Betsy's seventieth birthday party, which she has been meticulously planning for months. Every detail has been finalized: the invitations, flowers, entertainment, even the goody bags. But her mother keeps nudging her to add shrimp cocktail to the menu and to include three second cousins she left off the list.

"She's ninety-six, but she still rules," says Betsy, with a sigh and a shrug. "I don't even think of my mother as old."

Betsy knows she is lucky that her mother is still spry, getting by with only the help of a live-out housekeeper, and is not a burden to her daughter, except to tax her patience. Yet Betsy calls it "a bit strange" to be approaching seventy and still reduced to feeling like a little girl when her mother unfailingly questions her choices.

"Her favorite expression is 'What do you need that for?'" Betsy says. "Whether it's a food I'm serving or a chair I bought for the living room, she has a better idea." Betsy's mother is finally slowing down—she only plays poker twice a week now, down from her nightly game. Yet, as she climbs toward one hundred, she hasn't let up in poking around nearly every area of her senior-citizen daughter's life, from trivia like furniture and menu selection to larger family events and personal issues. Betsy is caught between feeling enormous devotion and enormous guilt at the same time. Lots of women circling age seventy are experiencing these mixed emotions; they are a new breed of seniors whose mothers, in their nineties, comprise the most rapidly growing segment of America's aging population. When boomer women start turning sixty-five in 2011, many of them will likely be dealing with feisty, vital moms. This extension of the life cycle enables mothers and daughters to enter an unprecedented passage of growing old together, savoring bonus years that are enriching—and educational—for both of them.

Jayne Karsten, an eighty-one-year-old high school teacher in Annapolis, says that she and her two daughters, ages fifty and fifty-two, talk about lots of topics now they never spoke of before: "The dialogue is deeper and different," says Karsten. "They have a new appreciation of the challenges each decade of childrearing brings on, so they see me through older eyes, with new respect. They see me as a survivor, and the fact that I made it through raising four good children gives them hope they can do it too.

"It's really a whole new passage of life for women," Karsten continues. "For instance, my oldest granddaughter is now getting married, and I lived to see the beauty of this ceremony and to experience her joy. And I could very well be alive to see my own daughter become a grandmother."

Treating our mothers right could pay off when we're Karsten's age and beyond. Children learn by example, and if we're nice to our moms, our kids are more likely to be kind to their elders, too. This is good news for those of us who want to be doted on by generations of descendants to come, which could be a substantial brood if statistics on aging continue to climb at the rate of the past century. In 1900, the average life expectancy in the United States was forty-seven years; in 2006, women are delivering first babies at that age. Some optimistic anti-aging experts predict that average life spans could exceed one hundred twenty before 2046.

The notion that we have the potential to rival the longevity of Galapagos turtles seems far-fetched. Yet, heart transplants and animal clones sounded like science fiction just thirty years ago. An age-busting pill would not surprise anyone. Preserving health through technology is a pressing priority for modern scientists, many of whom are baby boomers bent on beating their own clocks. So who knows what looms ahead?

What I do know from dozens of interviews with mature women is that as long as we're still our mothers' daughters, we are prone to behave like children—even when we become old enough to get our hips replaced. As Betsy's story illustrates, no matter what your age is, as long as your mother is still alive and in your face, you can remain stuck feeling like a little girl. To manage the shift into late midlife with a demanding, old mother it helps to tap into a basic Buddhist principle: Love her in the moment, and the rest will take care of itself. Noted psychologist Florence Wiedemann, a longtime devotee of Buddhism, offers her perspective later in this chapter on how dwelling fully in the present and letting go of past anguish make this last stage of being a daughter spiritually fortifying, even emancipating.

Here is more from Betsy, who is starting to organize a surprise ninety-seventh birthday celebration for her mother at the same time she is trying to keep her mom's nose out of her own upcoming birthday party.

Betsy's Story ✒

At ninety-six, my mother is still ruling our whole extended family. She really is. Like every mother, she's in everyone's business, and she worries about everything. My daughter and her family are on a vacation, and she keeps calling me to ask, "Have you heard from her? Do you think something is wrong?" Yet, she is so admirable in so many ways. At her age, she is still very up to date on styles, on the news, on books. And she is very opinionated and can intelligently discuss any issue. She reads the local newspaper, cover to cover, every day.

Really, she's like Auntie Mame. She's a very good-looking woman with blonde hair and a trim figure; we just took her shopping for my birthday party. You should see her in her new St. John's black and yellow suit. She worked for a long time as an accountant, and up until two years ago she did her own tax returns. Six younger women in her building have taken her under their wing, and she plays poker with them every Thursday night. She makes most of her own dinners, because her housekeeper leaves at 2 P.M. It's unbelievable, really, that she has been independent for this long.

Some days I leave my mother's apartment crying, because I can't bear the thought of losing her, which is going to happen soon. She's ninety-six after all. Then, after spending a whole weekend with her, I am ready to kill her. Not really, of course. All of my life, my mother wants to know everything that I'm doing, and that can diminish my sense of my own abilities. It is patronizing, and there are many, many days where I say to myself: "Betsy, you are about to be seventy years old. Why do you let her treat you like a child?" But, you know, as long as your mother is still alive, there is a big part of her that sees you as her little girl.

Lately, I do see a change in her. I do think she's consciously trying not to interfere so much in my life. The hardest part is that when she tells me how to do things, she is usually right. At last, she is realizing that I am old enough to make wise choices for myself. It's as if she has finally grown up to the idea that I am a grown up. That makes me happy. I also see other changes that are upsetting to me. She is definitely in a decline. For so long, I've had this vision of my mother as healthy. When my father died fifteen years ago, she was very strong throughout this ordeal. She never got hysterical. She quickly pulled herself together. And she stayed strong like that for years and years. The reality now is that she is increasingly helpless; she needs to grab someone's arm when she walks; she needs help putting on her shoes.

She used to be a fantastic dancer, tango and cha-cha, but now she's had a problem with ulcers on her legs. And her eyesight is starting to fail. But her knack for being controlling is still strong. I'm sure my kids would say I'm controlling too. It's actually impressive, that at her age, my mother is still busy telling everybody what to do, her two children, four grandchildren, and now she is involved with eight great-grandchildren. We expect it from her. I have had her so long I cannot imagine life without my mother. I call her at 11 P.M.; she's up until midnight. I say, "Hi Mom, how are you? Is everything OK?" And if I don't call my mother by 11 P.M., she calls me immediately and asks, "Are you all right?" I have been connecting with my mother every day of my life for seventy years.

I'm very afraid of her death. I don't like to think about it. When she goes, I'm next to go. Having my mother still alive, this is a cushion for me, knock wood. And I'm telling you, she is still very much alive. We all feel it.

My daughter in many ways is more patient with her than I am. She calls my mother on her cell phone almost every night on her way home from work. My mother loves it. She tells me, "Sometimes I will discuss things with Grandma that I don't talk about with you. And she's very forward-thinking and gives me good advice."

Growing up, I had a hard time talking to her about my problems. And we still have a tension in our relationship; I don't think that tension between a mother and a daughter ever really goes away. I'm near seventy and she's ninety-six, and we still have it. My mother still makes me angry. What mother doesn't?

Lately, I've been feeling guilty that I'm not spending more time with her. Even though we live only thirty minutes from each other and talk a lot by phone, I don't think I'm there for her as much as I should be. That's because I'm dancing as fast as I can for myself; this is a difficult stage of life; I mean, I am surrounded by illness and death. I want to live! I know she wants more of my time. I adore my mother. I am happy she is alive. I admit, however, that I am very selfish, and this is all that I am willing to give.

I work four days a week, and one of the reasons I keep this schedule is that I don't want to be always available to everybody who needs me. I want to continue to grow and develop myself. I direct operations at a nonprofit that serves adults with learning disabilities. And this work is very satisfying and challenging. I need this for me. And it's hard, because of the tugs in my heart that I should be taking care of other people in my family. But if I weren't selfish about staying engaged in my work, there would be a big void. And that can't happen, since I need to have my own life to fall back on when the people I love most aren't here anymore.

I'm the only woman I know my age who still has her mother. Not only is my mother here, she completely knows what's going on. But I always have this feeling that whatever

I have done for her, it's never enough in her eyes. My mother would have given up everything for her children. She was a very good mother in terms of devotion. And we are different. I have not devoted my whole life to my children. I haven't stopped working to take care of my family. My own development is too important to me. It's all I have in the end.

So things are good, and things are not so good. But that's the way life is, right? And you know what? I'm sure my daughters think I am very controlling too. I admit that it is very hard for me to keep my mouth shut; I'm probably more like my mother than I realize. And there's part of me that really likes that I still have a mother who tells me what to do. She tells our whole family what to do. And one important reason that she's still with us is that we allow her to, up to a point. She remains actively engaged in all of our lives. She is the undisputed matriarch of our family.

Making the family matriarch feel like the queen of her extended clan may actually help her live longer. Scientists point to loving relationships and staying physically active and mentally engaged as key components of successful aging. These common-sense strategies for maintaining vigor and clarity are echoed in the conclusions of a decade-long study of 1,350 seniors conducted by the MacArthur Foundation Research Network on Successful Aging. In their 1998 book, *Successful Aging*, which documents the study, authors John W. Rowe and Robert L. Kahn found that the central factors contributing to healthy mental and physical functioning in later years are social connectedness, exercise, and productivity. Playing poker with girlfriends counts.

"The research in aging shows that the more engaged you are in meaningful social relationships, the better you do health-wise," says Dr. Gene Cohen, the first director of the Center on Aging, Health & Humanities at George Washington University. He is also the former acting director of the National Institute on Aging, which is part of the U.S. National Institutes of Health.

"Spending time with loved ones has a positive effect on the immune system, boosting your protection against cancer and other diseases," Cohen continues. "Again, it's the simple issue of intimacy and frequency of contact that gives people the most mileage."

Although Betsy sometimes feels like a negligent daughter for not spending enough time with her mom, even her frequent phone contact is life giving. Betsy's nightly calls to check in, "Hi Mom. What's new? I love you," give her nonagenarian mother the comforting reminder that she is needed and she is not alone. Her daughter's love gives her life and a reason to keep going. According to Cohen, science is proving that seniors who are lonely and disengaged from meaningful relationships are more susceptible to diseases catalyzed by stress and depression. Whereas positive and repeated social connections boost the immunological response, prolonged and unremitting stress from loneliness can actually kill.

"There is no question that love promotes health," adds Cohen. "And the desire to repair relationships does increase as we age. The summing-up phase of life, a process of reviewing your life, starts in the late sixties and becomes very strong moving into the seventies and eighties. Summing up involves looking back at what is unfinished and what is unresolved in your closest relationships. Particularly with people in their eighties, there is a heightened desire to resolve any leftover conflict in their most intimate relationships. We are seeing a lot of psychological growth in people in their seventies and eighties; the ability to grow really never stops."

For my own mother, growing up meant refusing to cave to the loneliness of widowhood and instead starting over, as a saleswoman at Lord & Taylor. It was inspirational to witness her makeover from housewife into retail dynamo, dressed in outfits she used to wear only when she went to dinner parties with my father. And it has been excruciating to accept that an ageless, vibrant mother is deteriorating.

My older sister, Frances, and I were recently driving together along Chicago's Michigan Avenue, past Lord & Taylor, then past our mom's apartment building. We were silent and sad, and then we started talking about who we will be when she is gone—sisters forever, but nobody's daughters anymore.

An attorney with four children, ages nine to twenty-one, Frances lives thirty-five minutes from my mother. With our brother in California, and my family in Maryland, she bears the overwhelming burden of overseeing our mom's doctors and caregivers. Like me, she feels lucky to have been a daughter this long:

It has been wonderful for Mother to see my oldest children from birth through college. As I've grown older, I have been increasingly influenced by the diversity of her life. Most of my friends have mothers who come from the United States, and they were raised in somewhat homogeneous surroundings. Our mother is exotic and educational; she re-

gales everyone with stories of her life in Poland and her life as a hidden child in France.

The richness of her multicultural background adds a fundamental perspective to how I think and how I act. And this is something I've really grown to appreciate the older I get. At fifty-two, I am still impressed with how she's not afraid to speak her mind, how she's basically not afraid of anything. Even after the amputation, and wheelchair bound, she totally charms the doctors and nurses and catches them off-guard.

At the age of fifty-two, I still have a mother who gives me unconditional love. I have someone who actually cares about everything in my life, even the trivia. Mother still has such immense love in her eyes, even in her state of confusion.

People who lose their mothers in their teens or in their thirties were basically only daughters to their mothers. We've had the opportunity for something greater. Mother has become a peer; she is watching me grow old and has helped me along the way. I talk to Mother about being a mother. Her steady support forms the basis of my confidence. As I age, there is great comfort in having the person who cares most about my best interests as a resource. If I have an ability to be engaging with all types of people in any situation, that is largely from observing Mother all these years.

So with whom will I share my biggest joys when she is gone? While my husband and friends provide wonderful support, it's a mother who truly gets the greatest pleasure and pride from a child's accomplishments. It doesn't matter how old you are. Kids want their parents to see them excel. Kids want their parents to be proud of them. I don't think that ever goes away. We've been lucky for so long.

It strikes me again that when Nancy Friday published *My Mother/My Self* in 1977, women were not having conversations about how their mothers were coaching them through their fifties and sixties. Gazing at portraits of their mothers, frozen in time and smiling above the fireplaces, they were stirred into foggy memories of youthful exchanges and unresolved rifts. In that era, the average life span for women was seventy-six years. Today, many midlife daughters have very alive mothers to contend with—and an opportunity to grow old together, as confidantes, on equal ground. With aching joints and defiant children of our own, we now start to empathize and see eye to eye with the woman who may have once been the enemy. "The mirrors are everywhere," proclaimed fifty-year-old Rita in chapter 3, as she raises a teenage daughter who reminds her of the stunts she pulled on her mother long ago. Indeed, longevity and luck give us the gift of time to work it out with our mothers while they are still alive. Better this than thrashing in retro rage after her funeral.

"What we're really talking about is working it out with yourself," says Jungian psychologist Florence Wiedemann, coauthor of *Female Authority: Empowering Women through Psychotherapy.* Wiedemann blends the female archetypal consciousness of Carl Jung with a longtime devotion to Buddhism. She speaks of letting go of mother-rage and being lifted by an ancient sweep of benevolent matriarchal images from which every woman can draw, from *La Mer,* French for "the sea," to Demeter, the Greek goddess of the harvest. I find this notion to be placating as I stand on deathwatch with my own mom. Indeed, Wiedemann's wisdom—that the good mother resides within—can help all women cope when mothers pass away.

Here is more from the septuagenarian Wiedemann, mother of three sons and the grandmother of nine, who has been in practice for thirty-five years in her hometown of Dallas:

A woman is always caught in the powerful emotions and energy that connect her to a mother. Boys grow up and try and dis-identify with the mother. Girls can never get away from identifying with the mother, particularly as adult women. We look like her, we may start to act like her in some ways. Men can reject the feminine. Most women embrace the feminine, and at some point that must mean embracing the mother. We need completion with the mother, and some forgiveness, to grow up ourselves.

And here's where the Buddhism comes in: Forgiveness, in this sense, is accepting the Dukha, or the suffering, or the pain. You know, life is Dukha. Life is suffering. We can get over Dukha. Forgiving your mother means you stop wishing she were someone different, or that your life was something different. It is what it is. And from that acceptance, there comes an opening in your heart to truly grow up yourself, and to grow up together.

You have to stop blaming the mother for everything. I hear from patients who feel empty and angry; they don't feel any joyful desires. They are just mad, and it's all the mother's fault. And these are the women in their late forties who have been unable to create their own love relationships or have children, because they are imprisoned by this old anger. And maybe they did have mothers who didn't praise them at all or show love. But there are other mothers women can seek out, other women who care for us deeply, like aunts or teachers. And there is a great archetypal Great Mother of the earth that all daughters can connect to. Sit by the sea and feel loved and embraced by the sea, La Mer, the Mother who sent all of us out here. Water is the archetypal beginning of woman. We came out of the fluid-filled womb.

But that human, frail, imperfect mother we all have—she just isn't going to give everything to you, particularly as she gets older and more frail. So forgive her if she isn't the perfect Great Goddess. Or else you will never grow up.

No mother is the Great Goddess who is always good. Each of us is just an ordinary woman who tries to be as good as she can be. And at some point, we all fail. Know that your mother did the best that she could and get on with things. When a daughter can understand her mother's limits and imperfections, it can be very exciting and emancipating. You both get to be more real. Sometimes, this freedom doesn't come until a mother dies and the mirror is shattered. But it's best if you can shatter the mirror before her death by your own development, your own forgiveness of who she is, so you do individuate and become a separate self. The older you are, the easier this is to do.

There is nothing easy about the mother-daughter relationship. Some people really are rejected by their mothers. But I see many women who come out of horrible childhoods and do just fine, because they surround themselves with other loving people. In the end, you don't have to love your mother. But you do need to have a sense of completion to grow into a healthy, strong self. And a lot of it has to do with a spiritual shift that happens when you let go. In Buddhism, if you accept what is and do not get swirled up in a hateful past, you're home free.

Adult women today can have female authority, where one can develop herself fully and know her own goodness, beauty, power, and truth. And that woman who knows her own power can get to the place where she can be truly empathetic and feel her oneness with her mother, without being bound to her in an unhealthy way. Some mothers are better at letting go of the embedded daughter and allowing you to individuate. These mothers realize that you're a different creature, that you don't live in her time or in her shoes and that you're not necessarily going to be like her. Then, there are the other mothers who are not able to do that. They can't separate. This is where Jung's feminine archetypes come into play, in which there is a negative mother complex and a positive mother complex. The positive transforming mother releases the daughter to become who you are. The negative ones are devouring ones; they eat you alive.

Wiedemann refers me to a fat book by psychologist Erich Neumann called *The Great Mother* for a historical perspective on the symbolism of the Jungian feminine archetypes represented in mythology and ancient artifacts. What I find from Neumann, a student of Carl Jung, is that the modern daughters I interviewed echo the same polarity of maternal emotions as those portrayed throughout the ages. Since the time of ancient civilization, the Great Goddess Mother depicted in art and myth emerged as either extraordinarily good or extraordinarily terrifying. The transforming Greek earth goddess, Demeter, shines from the Good Mother end of

Jung's Archetypal Feminine, a range of traits that embody the instinctual, collective unconscious of what it means to be a woman. As provider of the harvest, Demeter is a bountiful source of fertility and nourishment, a reminder that the womb is where all life begins. Other positive feminine archetypes can be found in the effigies of mothers with suckling babies, such as the numerous renditions of the Madonna and the Egyptian goddess Isis peacefully nursing Horus.

The devouring symbols Neumann classifies as the Terrible Mother include the Indian goddess Kali, who wears a necklace of bones and wields a knife, and the snake-laden Medusa, with her petrifying stare. The Good Mother and the Terrible Mother threaded through ancient mythology come alive today in stories I hear from modern daughters. They speak of mothers as archangels and monsters, nurturing and devouring, adoring and hostile. Our mothers revitalize like the goddesses of sun and rain; they hiss and bite like Medusa's snakes. Our mothers cannot fix everything; mothers can be comforting, mothers can be mean, mothers kill, mothers die, just like everybody else.

Wiedemann continues:

Whether you had a loving Madonna or a devouring Medusa or a combination of the two, there is a primal attachment to the mother that is eternal. She is the original person who loved you. And of course there is the danger of becoming overly attached. I see women in their late forties who have too wonderful, too caring mothers who are the emotional center of their lives. They are both hanging onto each other too tightly. These daughters aren't married, they are working eighty hours a week, maybe they have a couple of dogs, but they aren't balanced, whole, fun people. In short, they aren't grown up. The positive mother transformation allows you to grow and become independent and strong on your own. The positive mother sets you free. In the end, it's up to the daughter to become whole and centered. She does this by becoming engaged in her own talents and passions, and by loving and being open to the Great Mother within and the Great Mother force in the world.

I hear terrible things that have happened in families, unforgivable acts. And some women cannot forgive. But in order to get to this sacred place of wholeness, you do need to have some empathy for the human mother who can never be perfect. You have to remember that your mother had her own disappointments with her mother. The Buddhists got it right. Stop pining and whining about what's not there and accept what is there. That means being content with a good-enough mother and not getting stuck in blaming her for not being ideal. Blame is a poison. Renouncing the blame allows your own desires to flourish. We are our mother's daughters, but we need to learn how to live fully in ourselves.

By being complete in yourself, you don't feel like you have to go back to your mother and list everything she did wrong. Don't do this to a ninety-year-old woman. That doesn't clear up anything. It's just going to make her madder.

Growing older with your mother, you don't just love the other, you are the other. She was a daughter and a wife and a mother, and you are too. She did what you're doing; she cooked all those meals, washed all those dishes, helped with all that homework. She was organized and intelligent and *responsible, even if she wasn't everything you desired. So give it up. Be Buddhist: Acknowledge the suffering and the pain, but don't get stuck in it.*

Wiedemann's expansive work with women has shown her that stewing in mother-rage can be a central block to a daughter's liberation and happiness. The daughters I spoke to put it this way: "If you can't forgive, at least forget." Indeed, the chemical reaction of hating your mother can poison your health and other love relationships—and make your mother's final years miserable for both of you. A fifty-two-year-old woman I know hasn't spoken to her mother for nearly two years, even though her mom was close to death twice during that time. Her brother leaves her phone messages, reminding her: "It isn't gonna be long. You better fix it while you can." This daughter flatly refuses to explain to her brother, her only sibling, or her mother what made her so angry in the first place. I called her mother, Greta, and spoke to a sad and sickly woman whose side of the story left me crying. Her words tell us what it feels like to be approaching your end and to have a daughter who isn't speaking to you.

Greta's Story

It's heartbreaking. We live in the same town. And my daughter doesn't talk to me. She is divorced from her husband, and the only way I can see my grandchildren is to go through him. So I don't see those kids much either.

Every place I go, I never stop searching the crowds. I think I'm going to see my daughter. And I think maybe this will be the time that she will come over to me. One day, I did see her in a store, and I started to go over to her but then stopped myself. I thought, "What will we talk about?" This rift probably started when her father was so sick fourteen years ago. I was oblivious to what my children needed at the time because I was consumed by his illness; he was paralyzed at the end. Then when she got divorced, it occurred to me that maybe she was needing something from me during that time that I didn't give her. But she has never tried to talk to me about our relationship, or even given me a chance to apologize for anything. She doesn't even speak to me anymore. No phone calls. No visits. Nothing.

I have been in the hospital twice with life-threatening blood clots, and she knew it and I never heard a word. Finally, I called her and I said to her, "What is the matter with you?" And she said to me, "Mother, I can't deal with this now," and hung up. That was months ago. I am seventy-seven years old. And I can't deal with this either, having no communication with my daughter. I talk to my son all the time; he is wonderful. But a son is a son, and a daughter is a daughter. One of the hardest parts of this is that I had a wonderful relationship with my mother. My mother and I were best friends. I catered to her every whim; Friday night we'd have dinner together. And I would see her every Sunday, long after my father died. I called her first thing in the morning and the last thing at night. Finally, she ended up moving in with me; I was so concerned about her as she got older, I just wanted her right next to me.

I remember the birth of my own daughter as if it were yesterday. After several miscarriages, I wanted a baby so desperately. Then, I had her. She was just gorgeous, china-blue eyes, a turned up nose. And she was so smart. She was reading at three years old. The sun rose and set on her. I tell you, I have no idea what went wrong. One day she told me, "Mom, you were never there for me," and instead of explaining, she disappeared. I know my daughter will someday live to regret this. Because, day after day, she is putting one nail after another into her mother's coffin. You know, if she had been abused or neglected, then I'd understand. But this is a girl who got everything she wanted. Maybe she had it too good.

I don't know how she feels, but I can tell you how I feel: I'm the poor mother who is missing out on seeing her grandchildren as much as she would like. It really is a very sad situation. I think about my daughter every day. It never leaves me. I have a child out there, alive, but it's as if she is dead in my life.

Greta would love to convince her daughter to attend a counseling session with her. But this daughter is not reachable; she doesn't return phone calls, does not respond to letters, and Greta is afraid to show up at her door. So all Greta can do is try her hardest to focus on the love she gets from her son, his wife, and their three small children. No mother should have to go through this, unless she committed murder. I wish I could introduce Greta's daughter to Janine, who was able to let go of her rage after being beaten with a horsewhip. I would tell her of my own past fury, about how the mother I have at fifty is much better than the mom I had at sixteen, and how relieved I am that I didn't blow my chance to love my mother fully. I challenge every midlife daughter still mad at her mom to consider this: What good is this old hate doing for you, for her, for your children, for your spouse, for anyone else you know?

Letting go of hating your mother is actually more selfish than selfless. Because you just may find, as I did when shaken awake after my mom lost her leg, that the woman who bore you still has a lot to teach you about courage and commitment and growing up at any age.

Don't miss out on this final act—it's the best part of all in the mother-daughter show. Listen hard and spill all while your aging mother is present and when change is still possible. I'm asking every question I was afraid to ask and talking very fast as my mother's short-term memory is fading. Closing the wounds takes backing off from a stubborn stand-off, sucking it up, and saying, "I'm sorry," even if you're not sorry one bit.

Who cares if you are right and your mother is wrong? It won't matter when she's dead. What matters is coming to a resolution, smoothing things out—now. Your mother will win anyhow, when she passes into heavenly peace while you are left behind simmering in guilt and rage. Making up in this lifetime makes you the winner. You get to reap the benefits of closure in the final chapter, rather than being stuck agonizing over what could have been had you worked harder on rewriting the ending. It took her mom's brush with a near-fatal illness for fifty-year-old Beth to "take responsibility for my relationship with my mother."

Beth's Story ❧

Beth is slicing an avocado on a teak cutting board in her kitchen in Tucson, Arizona. Sweaty from tennis, she is talking about her mom, who is recovering from heart surgery and finally doing well after a month in intensive care. The salad

Beth is making, with avocado, spinach, and smoked trout, is a recipe from her mother, an excellent cook.

During the months of her mother's illness and slow recovery, she has looked hard at their relationship, realizing she had often been "reactive and resentful." Beth is now "grown up and proactive" about taking the love she needs from her mother rather than waiting around to get it and ending up disappointed. Toying with a strand of turquoise beads around her neck, Beth describes her turnaround: "When my mom shuts a door, I open it and walk right in. I used to turn away. As I get older and stronger, I am not afraid to go in and try to get close to her. She doesn't always want that."

Beth's story is reminiscent of the basic advice a parent gives a child on how to get ahead: Don't wait for life to happen to you; you have to go out and make life happen.

What I remember most about my mom from when we were young is that she was so tidy all the time. You couldn't leave anything anywhere without it being picked up immediately. You leave a sweater for five minutes, and the sweater would be gone. And I remember at some point in my childhood, I said: "Mom, you know, people live here. You don't need to make this place look like there's no sign of life here."

And that's the way she is today. She's just very tidy; it's her way of keeping one area of her life under total control. I think the way she kept everything overly organized upset me as early as four years old. Because I have a very vivid memory of taking a stuffed animal and methodically ripping out all the stuffing, and there was stuffing everywhere. I got in trouble for that. I would do these sorts of very subtle devious things. Like in our living room, I would draw little pictures with Magic

Markers behind the couch and the chairs so you couldn't see them. I guess it was my way of destroying her order.

When I was about nine, my mom had broken her arm and she was resting in bed. She asked me to go downstairs and get her a banana. I used to like to squish my bananas before I ate them. She said: "Now don't smash the banana. I want it just like you find it." I got her a banana, and on my way upstairs to her room I remember just smashing it really hard in my hands so by the time I gave it to her it was mush. And she sent me to my room.

When I think about all this, I see that I was trying very hard to establish myself as someone very different from her. She was very orderly and very feminine. I was not into girly stuff, and I was kind of a mess. I always bit my fingernails. It drove her crazy. As we got older, my friends loved to play at our house because my mother was really physically active. She would help make these elaborate stages for us and we'd make costumes and do these musicals. My friends wished she were their mother. My mother was very slender and limber, and I felt awkward next to her. And she'd make these comments about me not being more graceful. Here, I'd be expressing myself by dancing around the house and feeling joy and abandon, and my mother's words would pop my bubble.

As the years went on, I began to excel at sports that she was good at, and it was very hard for her to lose to me. We had a tennis match about ten years ago that I will never forget. I was beating her, which is very difficult to do because she's so good. But instead of complimenting me, she said, "Oh now you're going to be so full of yourself."

I've gotten these messages over my lifetime, where she couldn't come right out and say something nice because she didn't want me to become conceited. Like she always needed to knock me down a notch. I don't fault her for it; she grew up with a mother who was very critical, and detached from her children. She never hugged them or said, "I love you." That's who my mother became; it was hard for her to say, "I love you"; she sort of dances around it.

But there were other ways she was openly caring. She is very domestic; she prepared beautiful food and set tables perfectly. She threw the most amazing birthday parties for us. She catered to me when I was sick. In many ways, she was a wonderful mother. She just didn't really know emotionally how to help me feel positive about myself. She never said, "Oh, you're so great." I wanted to know that she approved of me and that she was proud of me. I never had that feeling growing up. My hair wasn't right. My body wasn't right. My boyfriends weren't right. It's only, really, since I got into my forties that I've felt that my mother likes who I am.

I ended up not getting married. I know my mother's dream for me was that I would marry some handsome, rich guy. But I am single and childless. I certainly had plenty of boyfriends. Maybe I didn't trust being in love because love, as I knew it in my family, felt fickle, not lasting. I mean, my parents divorced after twenty-five years of marriage. Maybe there was a part of me that always knew whoever I chose would somehow disappoint my mother. It's as if I was always trying to please her but was never quite able to. It's only in the last couple of years that I finally feel as if my mother thinks I'm a good woman and a good daughter. After she got sick—she nearly died from heart failure—it gave me the chance to be a good daughter. It came out of nowhere; she had always been so athletic and healthy.

Until this time we weren't close emotionally. In fact, I once went four months without talking to her at all. I needed to totally disengage from her. I had been very depressed. My job wasn't going well. A lover of five years had just left. And I just needed space from her; I needed to focus on me, to listen to me instead of listening to her. And so I just cut off ties, and it was very hurtful to her. She couldn't understand why I needed to separate. During that period my sister called me and said: "Why are you doing this to Mom? You are really hurting her." But it really wasn't about her; it was about me.

So that was a big turning point between my mother and me. I became a stronger, separate self. I decided that I was in control of our relationship, and I started to be more proactive, with this attitude: "I'm going to take what I need from the relationship and not wait to get something." You have this expectation, and when you don't get it met, you just feel devastated. I wanted so many things from my mother that I wasn't getting that it just made me angry and sad. I kept going to the maternal well for years and years, and what I wanted wasn't there. So I turned it around. I decided to make it happen for myself. I finally said: "I don't want to be mad at her anymore. I don't want to be expecting her to fulfill these things anymore. I want a real relationship with my mom. And I'm going to go knocking on her door until I get it."

When she got so sick last year, it was kind of like, "OK, here's my chance." I was by her side throughout her entire ordeal, in the hospital from morning until night. I put my own job on hold to be with her. For a couple of weeks, the doctors told us that we might lose her. Here I was starting on a genuine relationship with my mother, and I was so afraid that she would die and that it would be too late for us. But she made it. She's home. She's exercising. Her close call really clarified for me exactly what it is I still need from my mother: I need to feel her love, even if she can't say it directly, and I need to express my love to her. I need to know that when she does die there's nothing more to say. I need to connect with her in a deeply loving way because that connection will support me when she's not around anymore.

One of her sickest days in the hospital, I said to her, "I love you, Mom." And she said, "I love me, too." That stung, but I kept pushing forward, and said back: "That's great that you love yourself, Mom. I just want you to know that I love you, too." She looked at me for a long time and said, "I love you, too." I wouldn't have done that before, to keep pushing. It used to be that when she shut a door, I would turn away. Now if I hit a door with her, I still walk right in and help myself to what I need. I am constantly visiting her and checking up on her, and sometimes she'll say, "You don't need to do this for me." I tell her right back: "Mom, I'm doing it for me. I need to see my mother."

As I age, my way of growing up with my mother is that I do not turn away from her when she hurts me; I stay right there and dig deeper in our relationship. Her way of growing is that she is finally able to give her daughter positive feedback. Last night I brought her barbequed chicken for dinner, her favorite, and when I left her house, she said: "I must have been a good mother to have such a wonderful daughter. Or, are you a wonderful daughter in spite of my not being a good mother?"

I am fifty, and I finally know that my mom thinks I'm wonderful. That will go a long way when she's gone.

Beth's bedside vigil, which gave her a sense of emotional completion, could very well have given her mother a physical boost, according to Dr. Jonathan Altschuler, a top Maryland cardiologist. This man, who specializes in angioplasty and other pioneering procedures that make it possible for seniors to survive heart ailments that used to kill them, notes a marked difference in recovery between those who have supportive families and those who don't.

"There is no doubt in my mind that a person's ability to heal is closely correlated with her support systems, whether that be from a spouse, a significant other, or from her children," Altschuler says. "We can fix things medically, but then the patients have to recover and heal on their own. The root of healing ultimately has to do with somebody's level of inner peace and contentment, and that comes from feeling like you're loved. If you know there are people around who care deeply about you, there's a much stronger will to live. I see these people all the time in their seventies and eighties, and they have this intense family support; the children are all there, hovering.

"Then you have these patients who have no one." He adds, "It's always interesting to me to measure those people who have loved ones anxiously waiting versus those who have been dropped off, and when you're done with their procedures, you wonder who to call. It does have an impact on the patient. You recover faster if there are people around to love you."

My mom is cloaked in love by her children and grandchildren, and I'm convinced that our love has extended her life. She willed herself to live until my son Isaac's Bar Mitzvah, and now she is talking about living until my twins Jack and Zane's Bar Mitzvah a year from now. Like Beth, I view my once-invincible mother hooked up to tubes in a hospital bed as an urgent wake-up call to make peace, now. Each time I leave her I cover her face in kisses as I used to do with my babies. Each time I leave I know the next time I see her she may be dead. Yesterday, when I left my mother in Northwestern Hospital, she was watching the wreckage from Hurricane Katrina on CNN. A year ago she would have been swearing at the television, cursing George Bush for his negligence. Now she stares mutely, often unable to remember our president's name.

As she hangs onto life by a flimsy filament, I am preparing for the final separation from my mother. Death is staring right at me, taunting, harsh, and real. Perhaps she'll surprise us all again—and live out the year. This bony woman with the clouded eyes who is putting up a noble fight is not the mother I'll remember when she's gone. I'll see a young Polish Jew with flashing eyes hiding out in France during World War II, putting up the fight of her life.

Four days before American troops moved in to liberate France, an informant told the police that the Catholic Helene Moreaux was really a Jew named Helen Steinberg. Two German guards came to my mother's apartment door in Montmartre and ordered her to accompany them. She fell to her knees, grabbed a kitchen knife, clutched their legs, and pleaded: "Here's a knife. If you take me, you must take me dead." She looked up from the floor and added: "Maybe you have a daughter my age. How would you like this done to your child?" The guards left.

She wasn't a cuddly mom, a cookie-baking mom. But she defied Hitler and death and loss and illness and forged ahead with enormous gusto. Her inconquerable spirit will steady me when she dies.

I am already grieving, in bursts, every day. I bury my head in my son Jack's silky hair, and I cry, awash with memories of being eleven like him and calling someone "Mommy." I remember being a defiant teen who wished my mom belonged to somebody else. I grieve each time I see her and she remembers her girlhood seventy years ago and nothing about yesterday. I grieve when I realize that when she goes, I will be an orphan, nobody's child.

When the end comes, I will not fall apart. Because I have already fallen apart and have started to put the pieces back together again. I am a fifty-year-old woman learning how to mother herself. I have internalized the best of my mother, and the bad stuff doesn't matter anymore. She lost her parents and siblings and my father and her leg, and she survived. Because of that legacy I will persevere when she is gone. And that is my mother's best gift to me—her guts. That, and a flat-link gold bracelet, a present from my father to his mother. When my grandmother died, my dad gave it to my mom. She gave it to me a year ago, and I haven't taken it off my right wrist.

As a child, I was mad because my mom didn't lay out her jewelry on her bed so we could ogle it together, as my girlfriends' mothers did. A lifetime later, I got her favorite bracelet, and we got each other's undying love.

chapter six

GUILT, GRIEF, AND MOVING ON

There is scarcely anything more difficult than to love one another.

—JACOB NEEDLEMAN,
A Little Book on Love

YOU'VE EXPERIENCED ALL SORTS OF DRAMAS so far, featuring an eclectic cast of women and all kinds of plots. There are mothers who hug too little and yell too much, and daughters with bulimia from emotional starvation. Annette's mother is sweeter than Donna Reed. Although each of these daughters has a unique history and set of circumstances, their collective voices resound with some common prescriptions for making peace with aging moms: Let go of the anger. Embrace her imperfections. Forgive her, even for unforgivable acts. Move on, into a mature relationship between equals, with a lowering of expectations and a surrendering of the heart.

Say "I love you, Mom" before it's too late.

"Give it up," advises psychologist Florence Wiedemann. "Acknowledge the suffering and the pain, but don't get stuck in it."

Alas, these simple, sage words don't work for every woman locked in a complicated struggle with her mother. Not every daughter is able to let go, embrace, forgive, and move on. As you will see in the stories to come, there are those who remain stuck in guilt and grief after their mothers are gone. They are suffering, not always in outwardly debilitating ways, but wistfully within. Gina, Claire, and Sophie are successful in their careers and are raising successful families. Yet there is sadness in their eyes, "should haves" in their minds, regrets in their hearts.

Their stories vary, but the core truth is the same: You have only one chance to get it right. Daughters who don't reach closure with their mothers are often left wondering, wishing, hurting. The wound can heal, but the process is slow and painful, and perhaps never complete. Indeed, a mother's iron grip may clench tightly long after her death, as a daughter's grief leads to guilt, and her guilt leads back to grief. These women speak of attempting to break loose from forceful mothers who dominated their daughters' emotions up until the very end—and in some cases, still do.

Gina's Story ✑

Getting over her late mother is still a work-in-progress for fifty-eight-year-old Gina, the editor of a celebrity magazine based in Los Angeles. Red Chanel glasses rest on top of her auburn hair, which is sleekly pulled back into a ponytail. She gets up frequently during the interview to approve fashion photos brought in by young assistants. Gina could pass for one of them, with her willowy frame draped in a silk-jersey pantsuit of forest green. However, she sits very still as she describes the confusing moments when her mother was dying, and instead of drawing closer to her mother, Gina let the years of pent-up anger push her away. In hindsight, she realizes, "I should have stayed with my mother and told her I loved her."

Although Gina leads an enviable life at the top of the publishing field, hers is a story of chronic pain over the kiss-and-make-up session that never happened. She talks of a mother who was loving on the surface yet failed to protect her in important ways. And in the end, Gina was too mad to melt. Today she warns other daughters blinded by accumulated anger to "make peace with your mother before she dies. Don't blow it the way I did."

My mother was totally involved with me. I was going to be the success that she wasn't. I was going to be the fulfillment of her hopes and dreams. But that was her fantasy. Because when it came down to focusing on the real me and what I really wanted and needed, she couldn't deal with that. Of course, I didn't figure that out till I was grown up. When I was little, I just adored her.

She was a hovering mother; she was always there yet I was always afraid she wouldn't be. We had this little mantra: When I left for school I would ask, "Will you be here when I get home?" And she would always say "yes." But sometimes she wasn't, so I learned not to quite trust her. I must have been very afraid that she would abandon me because otherwise why would I so compulsively ask, "Will you be here when I get home?" I have pictures of myself with her when I was about six years old, on her lap, cradled in her arms. I was too old to be clutching onto her that way. Yet, there are things I remember very fondly that we did together. We would sit together and do puzzles and number games and my homework. She had reddish, golden curls when she was young, and people used to see her and say, "Oh, that child has glorious hair." And so she had this thing about my hair, which was straight and brown. She made a whole set of curlers out of my father's old oxford-cloth shirts. She'd shred the shirts and stuff cotton in the pieces, put red ribbons on them, and roll them up into my hair to try and make it curly. I didn't mind this; I saw this as great hands-on attention. Looking back, I see that this was a way of not accepting me as I was.

I was a very late bloomer and I was very upset about it. The girls in my class started becoming very sexual starting in eighth grade, but I didn't. I didn't get my period until I was fifteen. So in eighth grade, I was flat as a board, and all this kissing and petting was going on. But who wanted to feel up a flat-chested girl? I complained that I had no breasts, so my mother went to Macy's and bought me a Hollywood Vasserette ice-blue satin va-va-voom bra. God knows what size it was. But it had these big pointy cups with great big falsies in them. And then she sent me to school. On Monday, I was washboard city. On Tuesday, I was Jane Russell.

The humiliation of that day is something I will never forget. The boys just went crazy. They were laughing and making catcalls, making faces like they were drinking milk from me. But this is what my mother was like; she wanted me to have breasts so she bought me breasts. If she could have bought me a period, she would have bought me a period.

As a child, when I would complain that I was unhappy or that things weren't working out for me, she would say, "Most people live lives of quiet desperation." Years later, when I went into therapy, my shrink said: "What? She said that? First off, it's nonsense. Most people don't live lives of quiet desperation. And it's certainly not something you want to hold up to your daughter as a goal."

It wasn't until I left home to go to college that I began to let go of illusions about my mother. I made a bunch of friends there and was feeling better about myself, less dependent on her. I also began to see other things that I had been blind to. I saw that my mother didn't protect me from my father, who was very seductive and very abusive. We had this Southern black lady who was a live-in maid, and she had more sense than either of my parents. She would take my father's hands off of my throat.

He would hit me or scream at me not because I was bad—I was a totally good girl who did very well in school. He would strike out at me because I disagreed with him. My mother would talk to her analyst about this, and the shrink would tell her, "Let them work it out together; it's their problem, not yours." So that's what I grew up with. She never intervened. She never protected me.

My father died when I was twenty-two, and a lot of changes started happening for me—in the way I saw my mother, in the way I was set free from her hold on me. As a symbol of this breaking loose I became seized by the idea of having long hair. I had always worn my hair very short, very masculine. But hardly a week after my father died, I went to Macy's—the same place my mother went to buy me breasts ten years earlier—and I bought this fake ponytail and somehow attached it to my short, scrunchy hair. It was as if now that my father was dead, I could be sexual. I could be a woman. So it was emancipating.

After my father died, my mother went back to college to get a masters in education and became a French teacher at my old high school. I admire her for that—to go out there and make it on her own. Yet, on the other hand, I was really, really angry with her. My dad was dead, the villain was gone, but I began to realize that she was just as much a villain in a way for not ever protecting me. And now, I'm like, "Screw you, lady." I graduate from college, I'm starting my first job. I'm having fun. I've got girlfriends. I've got boyfriends. I've got a fifth-floor walk-up apartment in Greenwich Village. And my mother is needy of me, but I'm not doing much for her, to be honest with you. And while I do give her credit for going to graduate school as a widow at fifty-two, by this time, I'm a butterfly. I'm sprung free from all of this.

At twenty-six, I married a very nice man who was loving and accepting. Someone stable and safe. We very much wanted a baby, but I had several miscarriages in the first few years. My mother was very sympathetic—that was her strong suit, being there when things were bad, being needed. Finally, after five years, I was delivering my first baby, and my mother somehow couldn't show up. Here I'm in the hospital, a moment of great rejoicing, and my mother couldn't bring herself to be there to greet her first grandchild. She saw my son two days later. I was very, very hurt. During the miscarriages, she was mommy perfect. She held my hand. She said all the right things. She was in prime motherhood during heavy-duty problems, but when it was joy for me, she wasn't there. Like she couldn't go shopping with me for a wedding gown or have anything to do with planning my wedding. I think she saw her function as being there for me during trouble. So it was good for me to be in trouble because then I could say: "Oh mommy, I'm so unhappy. Come and take care of me." And I got her full attention.

When my son was a year old my mother remarried. Another mad man, he was crazier than my father. The following Christmas my husband and I and our two-year-old son went to Florida, where my mother and her husband had moved. We arrived on Christmas Eve. We were tired from traveling and we got there and she had no dinner for us. Her husband didn't want her to do any cooking that night—he made a lot of lunatic rules for her—so we ended up at a cafeteria, with an exhausted and hungry two-year-old. I saw that my mother was catering to this man just like she had catered to my father.

I got madder and madder as I saw the truth: She had sacrificed me to my father. Somehow she had created an illusion of this blind devotion to me; here we were so intimate and I was constantly curling up in her arms and she did loving things for me. But all along she had been sacrificing me to his wishes, allowing my father to misbehave toward me. Her seductive good parts were in my face, but all this bad stuff was going on in the background. Something about being a wife and a mother myself—and seeing how she behaved with her new husband—brought it all together for me.

I wrote her a letter when I got back to New York, making a lot of accusations, rattling out my whole life. It was one of those really bad letters. I remember sitting at the typewriter and just pounding it out. She was devastated. But she didn't apologize. And really, there never was a reconciliation, which in retrospect is so sad for me. We never had that conversation we should have had. As the years went on, we were close, but the relationship was never quite satisfying for either of us again.

She did, however, turn out to be an excellent grandmother, and my children loved her. But she cut that short by her own hand. She had been a longtime smoker. She smoked so heavily that when she would go in the ocean for a swim, my father would come to the shore with a lit cigarette for her so she had her Chesterfield the minute she came out. The doctors told her if she didn't stop smoking that she would die. She would say, "Ha, ha, what do these doctors know?" Then she got emphysema. I would say to her, "If you don't stop smoking, I'm out of here. I'm not going to take care of you." It reminded me of when I was small and it was raining, she used to say, "If you don't put on your galoshes, you're going to get sick, and I'm not going to take care of you." But she always took care of me. I don't think I did so well with her.

I begged her to stop smoking, but she was in total denial. They put her on oxygen, and she thought, this is good because it will balance out the bad air from smoking with some good air. Finally, she decided to put herself into a nursing home, at the age of sixty-eight. I thought it was completely bizarre, but it was her choice, and she was sound of mind. She went into a physical decline, and she was very depressed; she died two years later. You know, after she died I never even scattered or buried her ashes. God knows what they did with those ashes. I mean, the level of my unexpressed anger was just so strong that the way I handled her death was just not to deal with it.

I was angry not just because of her smoking, but probably more from all of her behavior coming to a head. But I should have been there for her in the end; the illness was awful. Here was my mother, who had been so active, doing swan dives off the diving board just three years earlier, and now she's so sick and so alone. I would visit her often, leaving work in New York City at 5 P.M., then drive through traffic jams to this place in Long Island, and I would finally get there, and she would say, "Mrs. Jones's daughter was here all day." I felt very guilty. But I was in denial too. I diverted my attention to my job, to my kids, to my marriage, anything just to hang on. I was just very angry with her. By making herself ill, she had taken my mother away from me and taken away my children's grandmother.

I was in San Francisco on a business trip when the end came. I was blossoming. I had this terrific job. I was going to parties. I was in love with my life. And, to be honest, I was so relieved to be away from her and her illness that I didn't call her during this trip. I came back and she said, "Why didn't you call me?" I said, "I was so busy, Mom." And she died the next day. They called me in the middle of the night to tell me she was failing. I rode in the ambulance with her as she was being rushed to the emergency room.

She had been fine that day. Then she had an attack that night. I'm sure her disappointment with me had something to do with it. I stayed with her in the hospital for a while, but I just couldn't really bear to spend all night there. So I left and drove home to my family. In retrospect, there was my mother, critically ill, probably dying. How could I have not stayed there? It was crazy of me. It was not the right thing to do. Because she died that night, and I should have been there. She must have been terrified, alone like that, in and out of consciousness.

I went to work the day after she died because I didn't know where else to go. That's where my life was. That's where my close friends were. I think I thought: "Well, she did this to herself. She smoked herself to death. It didn't have to happen." Then, of course, the big question is, What would I have done if it weren't a self-imposed illness? Would I have made more sacrifices, been more empathetic? I don't know the answer.

What I do know is that I wish a conversation of closure had taken place. I'm sorry that we didn't embrace beautifully and that I didn't say: "Look, I know you made mistakes. Every mother makes mistakes. I love you anyway." I'm sorry I didn't say all of those things. I think it would have helped her, and helped me. I wish we had been able to talk in those last years. I would have wanted her to know the real me beyond her narcissistic fantasy of me. I think she was proud of me, but she had no idea who I really was. Maybe I didn't know who she really was.

Looking back, I think you have to put your own stuff aside and have that reconciliation. So I was right. She did bad stuff. Who cares? Then she died. So I think for me it would have been a random act of kindness to have been nicer to her in the end. When they called and said, "Well, what do you want us to do with the ashes?" I just told them to keep them. Why didn't I scatter them by the ocean she loved?

The week after the funeral I had the same impulse I had after my father's death, the need to express some kind of liberation. This time instead of long hair, I became seized with the need to get my ears pierced. When I was a kid and my friends were getting their ears pierced, my mother had been scornful. "That's for gypsies," she'd say. I accepted that and hadn't thought about pierced ears in all those years. But now, at the age of forty, with my mother gone, I suddenly felt this impulse. So I called an old friend and told her she had to drop everything and go with me. She held my hand while the jeweler pierced my ears and inserted tiny gold studs. My friend seemed to understand what this was about, even better than I did.

Today I tell my women friends that no matter what she did to you, even if she beat you, you don't serve yourself well by not having closure with your mother. You need to make your peace before she dies. I don't think I'm suffering horribly. But I know it would be better for me if I had forgiven her, forgiven myself, and set things right. I think about it a lot.

And in recent years, without really looking for it, I've found some redemption. When my grandchildren were born,

I came to realize that I am my mother's daughter, that she lives inside of me in the best way possible. When I sit on the couch playing "Go Fish" with my six-year-old grandson, I see my mother and me cuddled on her bed dressing paper dolls. When I braid my four-year-old granddaughter's long, straight hair, I can feel my mother putting those soft little curlers in my hair. It's not real closure—I still wish there had been one of those moments when we held hands and said: "I love you. I'm sorry." I believe by being a devoted grandmother I'm honoring my mother's memory. And that's been good for me.

Although impulsively getting her ears pierced suggests that her mother's death was emancipating, Gina is still weighted with regret. Yet, despite a conflicted relationship with a conflicted mother, she did manage to pull off the formidable feat of separating and growing into a confident, autonomous woman. The repercussions from a child's ability, or inability, to come out from under an oppressive mother have been a central subject of debate and study in psychology since Sigmund Freud began dissecting the human psyche in the nineteenth century. Psychologist Michael Kahn describes the conflict between wanting the comfort of mama and wanting freedom in his book *Basic Freud: Psychoanalytic Thought for the 21st Century*:

> Mother is the first caretaker for both boys and girls. This establishes a powerful bond, probably one that is never really broken. But this bond has a frightening aspect for the child: Relative to the helpless child, mother is overwhelmingly powerful, and the child's prospects of devel-

oping individuality and autonomy may be significantly threatened by the power of the mother.

On the one hand, the child wants contact with the mother and also her protection. On the other hand, there is a vast new world to be explored and the child yearns to feel powerful and free. There are more or less benign solutions to this conflict, but conflict it is, and one that teaches lasting lessons.

When her mother violated her daughter's need to be protected, Gina was not swayed by "benign solutions." Instead, she channeled her energy into a new world filled with exciting friends and career opportunities. But by not making up, she and her mother missed the chance to complete their relationship, to find closure that could have served them both well. The lesson in Gina's story is that if you don't do the grueling work of peacemaking before it's too late, you may spend the rest of your life kicking yourself. Listen to Gina. Hold your mother's hand. Let love overpower rage. Learn from your mother as she is dying.

As my own mother's days dwindle, I am finding that she still has a lot to teach her daughter, about grace, about forgetting the worst and remembering what is good between us. Every time I see her, I rub her hands and kiss her face all over: her forehead, her cheeks, her neck, as I used to nuzzle my babies. I say "I love you, I love you" over and over. I have dreams that she is dying and I miss my plane and can't be by her side. I want to be there when the blood throbs through her veins for the last time. This is the woman who held me when I took my first breaths.

The suffering that comes from losing a mother you're still fighting with is pain that doesn't altogether subside. "It's awful," says my artist neighbor Claire, whose mother died five years ago. "What's worse for me is that I don't think I ever loved my mother in the first place. That's what I live with."

Claire's Story

Puffs of pewter clouds are scattered across the sky after a thunderstorm in Annapolis, where Claire looks out over the Severn River and remembers the worst day of her life. She was twenty-four years old and waiting to be picked up for a date by a pro football player when she got a stunning phone call from her parents. Her nineteen-year-old sister, Gerry, had been in a freak hayride accident and was pronounced dead on arrival at a nearby hospital in Virginia. Claire was not their golden girl—that role was filled by her athletic sister. Claire wanted to live in Paris and paint and stay single and roam. Her younger sister was engaged to be married and hoped to have children right away, poised to fulfill her parents' dreams.

Drinking a Rolling Rock beer from the bottle, Claire is wearing a brown tank top splattered with yellow paint that reveals tight, toned arms from decades of tai chi and lugging her large-scale, abstract paintings. Now a sixty-three-year-old grandmother and an internationally known artist, she remembers the day "the good daughter died" more than forty years ago as if it were last week. Holding a fading snapshot of sixteen-year-old Gerry in a baseball uniform, Claire tells her story.

Talk about guilt. Why wasn't I the one who was killed? I was the irresponsible one. I was the one who was an artist. Gerry was going to be their heir, their traditional success story.

When we left the hospital, I kept saying, "Dad, pull over," because I had to throw up. Being sick to my stomach came not only from seeing my sister dead in a hospital; it also came because I realized that I was going to have to take her place. I would now have to provide my family with what my sister was going to provide them. She was already engaged. She was going to have children. They got along famously. To them, I was from another planet, this beatnik artist who wanted to live in Europe. It was just an awful, awful, confusing time for me, so many emotions swirling together.

There was an open casket at the funeral home, and they called and asked what we wanted to dress my sister in. I gave them this little baby blue Lanz outfit that she used to always steal from me. She went to college nearby at the University of Maryland, and she'd always take my clothes out of my closet and bring them out there. This was her favorite outfit to steal, so that's what we dressed her in. Everybody at that funeral parlor was just crying and crying and crying. A girl this age just isn't supposed to die. I had some college friends with me, and I looked back at my sister in her casket, and I just wanted to tuck her in. We shared a room, twin beds, and when I came in from a date, I always pulled the covers up around her neck and tucked her in. I went back to her and tried to do that, and the funeral director came up to me and scolded me, "You can't do that. You'll mess up her makeup." And my friends put up their elbows and kind of pushed her aside and said, "She can do anything she wants. This is her sister."

My mother and father never stopped crying. Never. They didn't even recognize that I was alive for about six months or so. It was just horrible. I never want to see another family have to go through that. It really changed the family dynamic. My mother used to pit the daughters against each other. She would say nasty things about Gerry to me, and nasty things about me to Gerry. Mother used to say to me: "Why can't you be more like Gerry? Why don't you play sports like Gerry?" And then she would say to Gerry, "Why can't you get straight A's like Claire?" You know, she was always sending the message, "Why can't you be like the other person?" instead of just saying, "I love you because you are you." She was always comparing us.

I knew that in my parents' eyes, I could never measure up to my sister. She was not as good as me in school, but she had something else. She was the doting daughter to my mother. She loved to go fishing with them, up and down the Potomac River on a motorboat. She was the star of the baseball team, and they loved going to her games. My mother loved babies, and Gerry was going to bring her babies.

My sister was going to be everything they ever wanted. And here I am; I was nothing like her. But, because of my sister, I got married and had children. I'm not sure, if my sister had lived, that I would have done that. Maybe I would be living in a garret in Paris had this not happened. Of course, now I realize that having children is the best thing I ever did. But when my sister died, I just felt very guilty and ended up assuming this other role. I felt like I had to hang around Washington for them. I felt that I had to make up for losing her.

My mother and I were never close, not when my sister was alive, not after she died. Then when Gerry was killed, I became the dutiful child and I took care of my mother, especially after she became a widow. I saw to her needs. But I never really forgave my mother for how she pitted us against each other or for how she smacked me around. Once I brought home a C-plus in algebra, and she beat me up. That was in eighth grade. She took that C-plus personally, like it was a reflection of her.

Eventually, I moved an hour outside of Washington to Annapolis. My brother moved to Virginia. My father died. And my widowed mother started making friends with some of the ladies in the neighborhood. I used to call them "Mother's Mafia," but they really helped open up her horizons again. She turned her house into a bed and breakfast and started making her own money for the first time in her life. She never stopped mourning Gerry, but she did start to be happier.

My mother and I never talked about my career as an artist, which was a very serious pursuit for me. I was doing well in the Washington area, although I always wondered what my career would have been like had I moved to Paris, the dream of my youth. And my mother and I never talked about my grief over my sister. I remained upset at my mother for many things, and I guess I just never got over it. I kind of bottled up this rage I felt, put on a smile, and performed as the good daughter my parents lost, even though it was very hard for me.

My children are now in their thirties, but when they were young I cared for them in a very different way than I was raised. For instance, my mother used to sit with us for hours going over our homework, and bad grades got bad punishment. My children ended up doing very well in school, but I would say to them: "If you want to get good grades, it should be to make yourselves feel good; it's not for me. I love you no matter what you do." I would never hit my children. Never.

When my mother died, I felt a huge surge of relief that I didn't have to deal with her anymore. We never did have closure; with our history, that would have been impossible. When my father died, I didn't cry. When my mother died, I didn't cry. But when my beloved black Lab died, I cried for days. She was very old and very ill, and my husband gave her an injection. And I was just holding her, and the 23rd Psalm came out of nowhere. I started reciting, "The Lord is my shepherd, I shall not want." There was an unconditional love with my dog that I did not achieve with my mother.

You know, dogs don't talk back to you. They are not demanding. They love you no matter what. My mother loved me on occasion. It wasn't a love that was substantial or consistent. You couldn't count on her love. Because of who she was, I am the person who thinks of life as if the glass is half empty, not half full. My way of coping was that my ballet teachers became my mothers. They adored me. They made me believe that I would become a professional dancer. Then I fell off a balcony and broke bones in my back, and that was the end of that. But those teachers and dancing provided me with this little haven where I was really loved and appreciated. Those of us who don't have warm mothers do seek out and find other mothers and other places where we are loved.

I have to admit I never really did love my mother. She was judgmental. She never said, "Claire, I love you no matter what." I am thankful for the creature comforts she provided, such as ballet. I went to summer camp for many years. Those were places I could feel loved. I treasured those eight weeks at camp each summer because there were people there who really cared about me. I remember when I was very young, and during rest hour my counselor Gracie would lie down on my blanket, and she would read to me and lazily stroke my hair. She was so kind. My mother never stroked my hair.

I can tell you that I stroked my kids' hair, big time. I kissed them all the time. I have tried to make up for my lack of good mothering, although it does stay with me, even at this age. I think about what could have been. I do think we should have had a conversation before she died about unfinished business between us. I really wish I had closure. I wish I had told her how much she meant to me. And I almost did that, at the very end of her life. But then I thought about what exactly she did mean to me, and there were bad feelings and words I did not want to express.

I wish that my sister were alive today, although I wasn't close to her either. Since my mother played us off each other, my sister and I were always at odds. Today when I look at pictures of us together in my old scrapbook, I know if she had lived we would have become good friends. I know we would have risen above my mother. But we didn't have the chance. And I certainly never had the chance, or the urge, to try and become real friends with my mother.

Some of the women we've met in previous chapters have demonstrated that friendship with our mothers can come if we are patient enough to meet each other totally and truth-fully. I think of the Haitian folktale, "One, My Darling, Come to Mama," retold by author Diane Wolkstein in *Magic Orange Tree*, in which the least-favored daughter comes through for her mother.

A woman has four daughters, loves the first three, and despises Philamandre, her fourth. When the woman brings food home for her children she sings:

One, my darling, come to Mama,
Two, my darling, come to Mama,
Three, my darling, come to Mama,
Stay, Philamandre, stay.
Stay where you are.

A devil comes and uses the song to steal the first three daughters away, leaving only Philamandre, who does stay where she is and therefore is not caught. The mother takes to the streets on a desperate search for her daughters. Mean-while, Philamandre has married the son of a king. Her ser-vants tell her of a beggar outside "who was in rags, and her wild hair, filled with droppings of birds, looked like branches of a tree," a woman who sings a song of Philamandre.

Realizing the poor beggar is her mother, Philamandre brings her into the palace, cleans her up, cuts her hair, and gives her new clothes. "Mama, the others are no more," she says. "But I am here. Look at me. I am Philamandre. You did not care for me, but I am here, and now I will take care of you."

The desire to take care of an ailing mother, even a diffi-cult one, can feel as natural as tending to a sick child. And that role reversal can lead to healing. As we tackle our own challenges with kids, marriage, and life in general and realize our mothers dealt with the same hard issues, we can also see them as mentors and as guides. My irrepressible mother, who was the queen of tough love and bravely faced adversity, gave me the tenacity to carry on no matter what obstacles are hurled my way. When I was young, I used to run away from her; she was an alien, nothing like me. Now with gray hair and sore joints, I am fortified when my mother appears in the mirror. She is my truth. I am my mother's daughter, and I see now that I always was.

Jane Fonda didn't meet her mother of truth (or her own true self) until the actress/activist was sixty-seven and her mom had been dead for more than five decades, killed by her own hand. In the first chapters of her eloquent memoir, *My Life So Far*, Fonda details her longing to understand her mother as a lens into herself. This after Fonda's lifelong, real-time drama with bulimia, unfaithful husbands, low sexual esteem, and a self-destructive desire to be perfect. She knew that to pen a solid autobiography, she had to face her mother, a process she had avoided for more than a half-century. When Frances Fonda committed suicide at the age of forty-two, Jane was only eleven, hardly an age to square off honestly with her mom, as many adult daughters are able to do.

Fonda grew from girl to woman believing her Connecticut blueblood mother was cold, weak, and dark. Researching her book, she uncovered a far different profile, a mom old friends described as a "lively, pleasure-loving, iconic rock of a woman." Fonda credits this discovery—"I was stunned. Mother? *A rock!*"—as an essential step toward her own completion and healing.

"I wished I could fold her in my arms, rock her, and tell her everything was all right, that I loved her and forgave her because now I understood," writes Fonda, after poring through her mother's past and discovering that she was molested as a young girl by the piano tuner and was spanked "often and hard" by an alcoholic father. This lonely, postmortem discovery amplifies the importance for women to meet, and comprehend, their true mothers while they are alive. We need to talk freely and listen hard. Finding peace within can only occur once you forge a peace with Mom.

Yet, even in peace, there can be an undercurrent of grief for a daughter who learns, as Fonda did, that a mother's life was one of unfulfilled dreams and sorrow. When Helene Krasnow told me she was happy overall with her life, she gave me an extraordinary gift: permission to be happy, too. Sophie's mother died with happiness eluding her, leaving her daughter to question whether she was entitled to have the happiness that her mother never achieved.

Sophie's Story ❧

Sophie, a delicate beauty of Brazilian descent, has a successful Web design business, two ambitious teenagers, and a twenty-year marriage. Yet, at the age of fifty-one, she struggles with haunting questions, years after her mother died with a broken heart over her lot in life. "Knowing that she wasn't ever really happy—this stays with me. How can I be happy?" asks Sophie.

Once a concert pianist acclaimed throughout South America, her mother, Lila, ended up playing the piano for shoppers at a Nordstrom's outside of Washington, D.C. Her long and loveless marriage ended in divorce. Holding a vintage portrait of the exotic Lila, with her black French twist spliced with gray, Sophie discusses what it felt like to be the daughter of a theatrical mother who presented a joyful face to the world but was melancholy offstage, at home. Lila counted on her daughter to fix her life, something no mother's child can do, something no person can do for anyone else. Four years after her mother's death, Sophie is left hoping she won't be left also, forever searching but never quite finding:

My mother did everything really passionately; she sang, she played piano, she loved to eat, she was a larger-than-life chanteuse who literally took over a room. She was vibrant, charmingly naughty, and had a fabulous sense of humor. But the irony was that she was actually a very sad woman who was disappointed with the hand that life had dealt her. She was unlucky in love, and ultimately unlucky professionally. I took it as my responsibility to fix her life. And that was something I was never able to do and always felt guilty about.

She met my father, an American soldier, when he came into a nightclub where she was performing, and they fell in love and soon got married. He was a scoundrel from day one. In Brazil, she was one of the top chanteuses in the country, written up in the paper constantly. But she left Brazil at the height of her career to be with my father, who had moved to Washington to pursue a business opportunity. They'd been separated for about four years, and her two children had stayed behind with her, my brother and me. And I think it was an enormous mistake to have left Brazil, because at that point, she had another man in her life whom she was very much in love with. She owned a successful nightclub. She was famous. Her family lived there. She was happy. Then my father lobbied so heavily to reunite the family, she thought she owed it to us to give us a life with both a mother and father. So this supreme sacrifice was really made for her children. And I think I've always felt guilty about that, that my brother and I were somehow responsible for her unhappiness.

I often wonder what our life would be like if we had stayed in Brazil and not moved to the suburbs of Washington. I am certain my mother would have been much happier. Here was this very flamboyant Brazilian beauty stuck in suburban Washington. She used to be the Grand Dame of Brazil. And she was never able to reclaim that status in the States, even though she did perform in fine hotels throughout the Washington area.

So my memories of my mother are quite different from those of my girlfriends: While most mothers were busy getting dinner ready for their children, my mother would be in her bedroom putting on makeup and doing up her hair in a French twist, putting on a cocktail dress, and getting ready to go out for the evening to perform somewhere. This was her ritual for as long as I can remember. I mean, my mother was no June Cleaver. Here she would be leaving the house at 5 P.M. with rhinestone earrings on. And we'd be left with her mother, my grandmother from Hungary, who moved to the States with us and spoke not one word of English.

Over the years, my mother grew more depressed. In her situation, who wouldn't be? She had faced this fork in the road: to stay in the heart of this incredibly cosmopolitan life in São Paulo or to leave. And she took the wrong turn. I was always struck by the fact that she gave up her whole life there for us. By the time I was fourteen, my parents divorced, so here was another stroke of bad luck—she came to the States to give us a father, and he ended up out of our house.

If you met my mother, you would never imagine she was a sad woman. She was vivacious and incredibly warm and very funny. And she was motherly and very physical with me, hugging and kissing. But even though she was clearly my parent, I always had this sense of obligation that I needed to protect her. I felt that since she had done so much for us, I owed her something, something kind of indefinable. My mother was very needy, and nothing I did could fill that void in her life. At the same time, she adored me. She was absolutely the defining character in who I became, and it started when I was young.

The fact that she had such a big personality and was always on stage reinforced my shyness. Because of who she was, there was a sense when I was young that it was sweet and adorable to be quiet and demure, and let her shine. I was patted on the head for my shyness; the alternative would have been to compete with her, and that would have been fireworks. She was just so strong that I chose to be different.

Frankly, I felt weak around her well into adulthood, and then I started to assert myself more, which actually created conflict between us. My first big statement was to move out of her house, which you didn't do in her culture. My grandmother had lived with us until the day she died. But after commuting to college for a year, I finally moved out of the house at the age of nineteen. Then I took it one step further, and I moved to Boston for work. And my mother would make these classic comments to me, like how she calculated how many times before she died she would probably see me, based on the fact that we were only seeing each other four times a year. Was I running away from her? Maybe. I needed to define myself at a distance from her.

Eventually, after many years, I did move back to Maryland, about an hour away from her home in Bethesda. I felt that I needed to be near her again. I actually missed the web of my family. I wanted to see her with some regularity, and part of it was guilt. But much of it was a genuine love and affection for her; I wasn't just being the dutiful daughter. After I started to see my mother again I realized that though I loved her, I hated how she could make me feel when she burdened me with her troubles. While I was trying to run my own family, which now included two children, I was always getting pulled in her direction. Eventually, her health really started to deteriorate. She had high blood pressure and diabetes. And in 1998, she died, at seventy-eight, after being stricken with an aneurysm in the brain while playing piano at a Nordstrom store. Thinking of her final days makes me very sad; she should have been playing in Carnegie Hall. It's like those aging movie stars who you see selling toothpaste in TV commercials. This was my mother's Crest commercial, playing hotels and stores—although at Nordstrom's she had a group of loyal fans who came and sat by her.

After she collapsed at the piano, she was flown to the hospital. A friend from Nordstrom called us and we rushed over. We were fortunate when we arrived because she still had some clarity and consciousness. She was able to tell me and my brother: "I'm so lucky I have you children. I love you two so much." And we were able to have this really wonderful moment of closure with our mother. Two days later, this would not have been possible, because there was swelling in her brain and she became gravely ill. So this was one of the last times we spoke to my mother or heard her voice, even though she hung on for almost twelve more weeks, most of it spent on a ventilator.

It was horrible because throughout that time there was no telling what she was aware of, and she couldn't talk because of the breathing tube. There were no precise instructions in her will, but she had always said to me: "Don't put me in a nursing home. Don't let them put tubes in me. When it's my time, give me a glass of Dom Perignon with arsenic in it." It was a difficult time for us, trying to decide how to handle the doctors and not really being clear how far to go with drugs and other surgeries. So we just felt our way along, hoping we were making the right choices for her, doing what she would have wanted us to do.

Then we had this moment of divine intervention that I am forever grateful for. My mom's eyes seemed to show that she was giving up, that she had no desire to go on. And I looked at her, and for the first time in weeks she made direct eye contact with me. I looked right at her and asked, "Mom, are you mad at me?" I was so afraid that she was upset with me, thinking, "How can my daughter be letting those doctors do all these things to me?" And my mom shook her head firmly with a "no." What a gift. If we hadn't had that moment of clarity, I always would have worried that I didn't do what my mother wanted me to do at the very end.

She died how she lived. It was very theatrical to collapse at the piano, doing something she was passionate about. I am now fifty-one, and my mother has been gone five years.

I understand her better all the time as I get older and reach certain milestones in my life. My second child is going off to college next year, and I'm thinking how it must have felt for my mother when I suddenly left home, and she was alone.

I miss my mother dearly. What I don't miss is how easily she could make me cry. I would get off the phone with her, and I'd bury my face in my hands, and I would say to my husband: "I don't know what to do with her. She's unhappy and I can't fix it for her." And this guilt would just eat me up. She had professional disappointment. She had romantic disappointments. She had health issues. And to see her suffer and not be able to do anything about it—but her expecting me to—just pulled me apart.

I always felt totally loved by my mother. But I knew that nothing I did could ever fix her life or live up to the sacrifices she made for me. I know that I'm a separate person; her history was so profoundly different from mine. But there are undertones of her sadness that have definitely colored who I am. I watched this incredible beauty with enormous talent who had the potential for a grand, joyful life fall into boredom and depression in suburbia. And it does leave me wondering: If this extraordinary, glamorous woman couldn't pull off happiness, what are my chances? I am excited about the next stage of my life, now that the children have left home, but I struggle, in some ways, as my mother did, with moments of discouragement. I understand my mother's depression—maybe through osmosis.

It can be hard to attain joy having witnessed the ups and downs of my mother, the constant shift of clouds and sun. In a way, I do feel guilty being happy. I do have a certain contentment that she didn't have. And I have a good marriage, *something my mother never experienced. But I have yet to realize my full potential or real passion. That is probably my biggest battle, and the biggest question for me: Is it OK for me to find happiness when it eluded her? Can I have what my mother didn't have?*

These questions gnaw at Sophie, yet because she did experience closure, she is released from relentless grief. This daughter can't beat herself up, because she did everything she could, in her mother's life and in her mother's death, to serve her with compassion and devotion.

This Sunday is Mother's Day, and I am ripped up inside, as Gina must have felt when she chose to go to her family instead of staying with her dying mother. Should I fly to Chicago to be with my mother to celebrate what is probably her last Mother's Day? Or should I stay in Annapolis with my boys, who were whispering at the breakfast table this morning about pottery dishes they want to buy me as a gift? I go to Chicago, my third trip this month.

My mother's face is chalky, one eye is swollen shut, and she is refusing all food except for over-easy eggs on toast. She is tired and in a bad mood, as anyone would be in her position. I remember her, not that long ago, rushing out the door, dressed in a red blazer with gold buttons, her face ruddy, off to work at Lord & Taylor. Today she wears a black terrycloth jogging suit and will never stand on her own again. She is too weak to try and maneuver with her prosthesis, a flesh-toned replica of her other leg that is leaning on the wall behind her.

I look at her left pant leg, which dangles over her stump. And I move in closer, to kiss her on her cheek, which is all bone and not dimpled and fleshy like it used to be. The final chapter is here, and the final page is coming. Our love is clear and expressed, and I am ready for her to die when she is ready to let go. I hug her, and she is so frail that it feels as if she will shatter. Yet her Shalimar scent is as strong and enveloping as her arms once were.

Long after my mother is gone, a whiff of Shalimar will bring her back, and she will be walking toward me, on two legs, and her face will be rosy and full. Today, at fifty, I don't need to be mothered. But I will always need to know that my mother loved me, and to know that my mother knew that I loved her.

chapter seven

REBIRTH AFTER DEATH

I am not afraid to die. I'll go to sleep,
and that's it. I have loved this life.

— HELENE KRASNOW

I AM SITTING ON MY MOTHER'S HOSPITAL BED. Her eyes are closed and her skin is like cellophane, exposing a lattice of bright blue veins. She is ready to die and not ready to die, telling my father—who died twenty years ago—"Teddy, I don't want to go yet" and asking me, "Do you need me anymore?" I say, "Mom, I love you, but I don't need you anymore."

The first part is true; the second part I'm working on. I want her to feel released from the tug of maternal duty, to bust loose from her withered body and regain her surefootedness as she is transported to her husband, father, mother, sister, and brother—long-deceased family members she has spoken to every day for the past two months with eerie clarity. She tells my father, "Teddy, you look different." She laughs aloud when she sees her brother, who died sixty-five years ago: "What did you do to your hair?"

Her doctor instructs us to "bring her down to earth from the fairy-tale castle" when she has conversations with dead people, to tell her sharply: "Mom, today is Wednesday, October 4, 2005. You are in the hospital. Your husband died in 1986." But I totally disagree with him. I hear her conversations with these people who are alive to her, and it is soothing to me. Her caregiver, Donna, reports that she will abruptly sit up and cry out, "Teddy is here!" Then she lifts her hand from under her white cotton blanket and curls it around his invisible hand, fingers arched and tendons taut as if she were actually holding on. Other nights she will say, "I am going home to my Mommy," and this is the best news of all—for her. What I will do when my own mommy is gone is my problem to grapple with, until I join her again.

So instead of following doctor's orders, I respond to her heavenly dispatches with, "Isn't it great, Mom? You will never be alone. If you go there, there are people waiting for you who love you. If you stay here, you'll be with your kids and grandkids. You can't lose." I smile, kiss her, and then fly out the door to sob.

As my mother is making the transition, watched over by loved ones on both sides, I am reminded of the words of Elisabeth Kubler-Ross, whose remarkable work with the terminally ill, chronicled in her book *On Death and Dying*, helped pioneer the hospice movement. For a UPI profile, I spent a day interviewing Kubler-Ross on her 250-acre farm in the Shenandoah hills of Virginia. After documenting the last breaths of more than twenty thousand dying people, Kubler-Ross assured me that she believed unflinchingly in an afterlife, even though many physicians thought she was crazy.

"I never worked with a dying child who didn't mention somebody waiting who preceded them in death," said Kubler-Ross, who died in August 2004. Kubler-Ross picked up an orange velour caterpillar from a basket on the floor. "This is what I show dying children. I tell them, 'Your body is just a caterpillar. When you die, the caterpillar will release the butterfly.'" She reached into the caterpillar's belly and pulled out a tiny monarch butterfly. "I tell them, 'The butterfly is the immortal part of the human being that flies up.'" She looked at me with burning intensity: "You don't think this life is all there is, do you?"

I do not. I believe another world beckons and is filled with familiar faces and kindred spirits. It's a tremendous relief to know the end isn't necessarily The End, when your mother is dying and your stomach is knotted because you are afraid for her and afraid for yourself. So my fear is tempered by exaltation. My mom is going to a family reunion. And I will find solace in my husband, sons, girlfriends, God, and in my certainty that I will see my mother again, possibly with a new hairdo. She is going but leaves behind our tangled history, an anchor that nobody can ever take away. This melding of my mother into me makes her last days oddly exhilarating.

I am bracing myself for her imminent death, rehearsing my response to the moment of impact. It's a feeble charade, I know. A daughter cannot know the depth of her loss until death is real. My friend Patti lost her eighty-five-year-old mother two months ago. We go to the gym together on Thursday mornings, and the week after her mom died we are eating bacon and scrambled eggs after our workout. I am talking about how well I'm preparing myself for the inevitable. Patti puts her fork down and asks me pointedly: "Do you really think you're ready? It's bigger than you think." Patti's way of dealing with the deteriorating condition of her mother, who lived nearby in a retirement community, was to concentrate on the moment, making every visit a celebration. Patti recalls:

My goal in her last months was just to do fun things and not dwell in sadness. One day, I would bring over a Katherine Hepburn–Spencer Tracy movie, and we'd watch it together. Another day I'd bring over pictures of her grandsons. Or we'd go to Chico's to shop and I'd get her something she loved. Every day I'd try to give her something to look forward to. Every day I wanted to make her laugh.

She's been gone two months, and I'll tell you what I miss the most, what has hit me the hardest: It's that phone call I want to make and say, "Mom, guess what happened today?" Because your mother is the one person who thinks what you did was the most incredible thing in the world. This is the person who honors everything you do. It's your mother. Not your husband. Not your children. And now that's gone. A time of my life, and a way of life, is over.

I used to call her and say: "Mom, get dressed. Let's go to lunch and go shopping. I want to buy you something today." It would give me such pleasure to get my mother some clothes she loved. I'll never do that again.

That's why I am asking you: "Are you really ready? Do you really know what it is that you are going to be missing?" More than just missing your mother and the phone calls and little things that remind you of her, this chain is now broken and can never be replaced.

I find myself looking through all her pictures, over and over. And I see her as a young woman and with my father when they were first married. There is a smile on her face, her eyes are bright; her life is full and forming. And it's over. Your mother is the most valuable person in your life, even if the relationship isn't always healthy. She guides the way you think. She makes you understand what it takes to be a mother to your own children. She loves you without condition. My mother knew me so well, even better than I know myself. Who will ever know me this well? Who can I talk to like I talked to her? That's the huge sadness I just didn't expect.

Yet, when she passed on, I was left with the best of her. So, in many ways I am growing in ways I have never experienced before. And I look forward to this next phase of my own life with that life force of my mother behind me and in me.

Other motherless daughters also spoke of a prism of emotions that continue to radiate through them for weeks and years after the funeral. Women who feel as if they "blew it" in the end, like Gina, have knots of grief that are impossible to knead out. Those who create loving finales speak of dramatic rebirths, as their mother's legacies and dreams are folded into their own spirits and ambitions. New York schoolteacher Erica, who outed her homosexuality at the same time her mother confessed her adultery, is one daughter who is surging with life after her mother's death. Because their closure was clean and complete, Erica is able to soar without guilt into a bold awakening, as an independent woman accountable only to herself. This clearheaded revival comes from the knowledge that not only did she treat her mother right in life but she also gave her a proper send-off:.

As she lay dying, I never left her side. I talked and I sang and I read to her. I fed her and I washed her and moisturized her swollen body. I held her hand, tears streaming down my face as she moaned in pain, and she slipped away from me. I stroked her hair and whispered in her ear that it was okay to let go if she couldn't take it anymore. I stood and watched the heart monitor slow down, and then finally, finally, stop. We motioned back the medical staff that ran to resuscitate her; my mother wanted no heroic measures. My brother and I held each other, crying. The only person who had known us every moment of our lives, who loved us so fiercely, was gone.

It is a weird feeling not to have parents anymore, but especially not to have a mom. I learned that there is a secret society of women who have lost their mothers as adults. These older daughters have come up to me and shared the most intimate details about their mother's last moments and their regrets about what they wished they had done. One woman told me: "It gets better, but you never get over it. It's been twenty years, but I miss my mother every day."

I, too, miss my mother every day. I think about her constantly. And yet, to be honest, I feel an incredible freedom now that she's gone. I can do whatever I want, and there is no one left whose opinion I care about.

As other daughters in this book attest, a mother leaves, but she never leaves. Erica sees her mother in the mirror; they have the same "crinkly eyes." Like Patti, she still reaches for the telephone to share her latest news. The resurrected daughter, post-mom, may feel buoyant, but she is never again totally whole. Gone is the woman who, whether it be true or not, personifies comfort and security. French author Simone de Beauvoir alludes to this spectrum of conflicting emotions in her book *A Very Easy Death*, which recounts her mother's long illness and ultimate passing. This stalwart of feminism writes tenderly in her tribute to an oppressive mother she loved, hated, and cared for, in her words, with "intensity and simplicity," as she was failing.

De Beauvoir atoned for the friction between them by being a vigilant daughter who exhibited "obstinate watchfulness" throughout her mother's hospitalization, paving the way for an easy death, what every family wants. Even with the peace of resolution, the author was still shocked at the residual turmoil in her heart: "Why did my mother's death shake me so deeply? . . . my sorrow broke out in a way that I had not foreseen. When someone you love dies, you pay for the sin of outliving her with a thousand piecing regrets. Her death brings to light her unique quality; she grows as vast as the world that her absence annihilates for her."

I already feel my mother's absence although she is still here. My larger-than-life mother is moving out of my world and into her own, one that is filled with late ancestors who are welcoming her. My mother gave this world her best shot, defying the odds to survive time and time again. As she straddles both worlds, I am soaking in any last lessons she has to offer, about grace and having the courage to hold on until you simply can't anymore. I ask my mom about her own fear of dying, and she brushes it off: "I'm not afraid of dying. I will go to sleep, and that's it. When it's my time, goodbye. I have loved this life." I think of my mother losing her own mother when she was just a teenager. If she survived her mother's death so young, certainly I can survive at fifty.

It's not any easier as a daughter creeps into old age herself, says sixty-three-year-old Juanita, who never left her mother's house on Chicago's South Side, raising her own two children there with her husband. Her mom, Ann, died recently at the age of ninety, and the emptiness in her home and her heart is overwhelming. An only child, Juanita was her mother's best friend, and in Ann's final years, when she was suffering from Alzheimer's, Juanita was her mother's nurse. Now a grandmother herself, Juanita cannot separate from the mom she called "Mother Dear," a woman who cleaned houses and department store ladies' rooms for more than sixty years. Juanita reflects on both the peace and loneliness she now feels, in the house where she was born and where her mother died:

Oh, I cried and I cried when she passed. But I am so peaceful because I know I did everything I could do for the person that I loved so much. She died right in her bed, and I took care of her myself, throughout her Alzheimer's sickness. I didn't want anybody cleaning her body or wiping her bottom but me. On the evening she died, she felt good, but she didn't want any food. She said, "Juanita, just bring a bottle of strawberry Boost." I fed her at a quarter to six, got her cleaned up, propped her up good with pillows, and she was very comfortable. She was talking like she normally did.

I said, "Mother Dear, I'm going to watch Wheel of Fortune, and I'll turn it on for you too." At twenty minutes to seven, I looked at the clock, and something got me off the sofa to check on my mother. She looked distressed, and when I asked her what was wrong, she couldn't talk. Not one word. I said, "Mother Dear, do you want ginger ale?" Finally, she said in a whisper, "No, Juanita." Then she turned her head and looked up to the heavens, and she took the deepest breath. Her skin color is medium brown, but her face had gotten pitch black. I started screaming for my husband. I knew she was dying. I got a pan of cold water and kept sponging her down, but she never responded.

Since that day, her spirit lives inside of me. My daughter was driving with me in the car the other day, and she looked up at me and said, "Oh, Mama, you're looking so much like your Mother Dear now." And I just broke down into tears. I sure loved my mother. I have become her, as far as her personality, her style of cooking, her moral values.

I'm so happy I got to care for my mother. When daughters are upset about their mothers' deaths, it's often because they haven't done what they were supposed to do, which is to love their mothers. To give them the most time that they can. That's what I did, even the cleaning of her body. No one wiped her down but me. I went on retirement early to take care of my mother, once her memory started fading.

I feel stronger than ever now that she's gone because I know she is at peace. She would say, "You know Juanita, I'm really getting tired." Sometimes I'd ask her, "Mother Dear, *are you ready to go?" And she would say to me, "Juanita, I don't want to die." She died when she was ready, and now she lives on in me. I did everything I could for my mother. She was my life. And it was exhausting for me, but I wouldn't have had it any other way.*

I was looking really tired one day, and one lady at church said to me: "Oh Juanita. You look horrible. What is wrong with you?" And I told her that the reason I look horrible is because I'm putting all my time into my mother. She said to me, "Why don't you have someone else do it?" And I told her that nobody else loves my mother like I do.

Juanita talks about daughters feeling bad about their mothers' deaths if they don't do what they're supposed to do—that is, lavish them with love and attention. Most of the women I spoke with did not assume the role of round-the-clock nurse as Juanita did; nor did they quit their jobs to be full-time caregivers. Yet every woman who buried a mother agreed that how they acted at the very end has turned out to be either healing or haunting.

Adrienne is a forty-four-year-old video production artist who lives in St. Louis. When her mother was on her deathbed four years ago, she bid her daughter a brazen farewell by flipping her the bird. Yet, Adrienne's confusion and shock were short-lived, dissipated by a mystical dream that turned the enemy mother into a beloved spiritual comrade.

Adrienne's Story 🌿

Adrienne is grabbing a pitcher of orange juice from the refrigerator in her condominium in urban St. Louis. Wrapped in a white terrycloth Ralph Lauren robe, she is five-foot-nine with the sinewy body of a model, her profession during the 1980s. Evi Adrienne, her namesake mother, was also a model, working as a Robert Powers girl in New York runway shows in the 1950s. While her teenage daughter, Mackenzie, sleeps upstairs, Adrienne shares a story of redemption with an estranged mother with whom she shared not only her name but also an "inner rebel" personality:

My childhood was enchanted in many ways. I grew up on the Chesapeake Bay, and I enjoyed a lot of beauty and freedom in nature at a very young age. From the outside looking in, our house looked warm and cozy. But from the inside, the relationships were cold. I've been hurt. I've been dark. I've felt abandoned and banished from my parents' kingdom. But I don't feel any rage now. Strangely, my mother's death has been great for our relationship. It is puzzling and beautiful to me, after a lifetime of being estranged.

Although we weren't close, I always felt a kinship to my mother, because I saw her rebel nature, which she passed on to me. The difference was she didn't act on hers. Instead, she chose to fulfill the role of dutiful wife and surrendered to my strict father, who came from a military background. Her inner rebel and feminist instinct would come across in quiet ways. If we were watching a movie with nudity and sex, she would express distaste that "a woman can be exposed in a movie, but why don't you ever see a male's private parts?" My mother didn't marry until she was twenty-nine, another sign of her rebel nature. She had a good, long time to be independent, and used to travel to Europe. She was the one who arranged for me to have a private meeting with Eileen

Ford in New York, which eventually led to a career in modeling. And that meant lots of travel and independence for me, as well.

My sister is nine years older, and my brother is five years older, so I lived alone with my parents for a large part of my life. My father tried to dictate my actions, and my mother went along with him, as did most compliant 1950s housewives. And I became very rebellious. I would take out the car without asking. We lived on the water, so I would take off in our Boston Whaler. Later, I would get on planes and travel far and often. Actually, my lifelong wanderlust was inspired by wanting to get away from my parents. I was running from their rules and the complete lack of emotional connection in our house. Tears were not allowed. Compassion was not available. If you were upset, you were told basically to "buck up and deal with it."

All I remember is not ever wanting to talk to my mother about anything personal. I developed very late; I didn't start menstruating until I was seventeen, and I looked like a runt until my junior year in high school, a tiny, scrawny thing with bird legs. I couldn't talk to my mother about the emotional part of this; she was only concerned from a practical sense: Her daughter doesn't have a period. So she took me to the doctor and he prescribed some pills to induce my period. It was like taking a car in to be serviced.

After two years of college, I started flitting around the country and the world, from Florida, to San Francisco, to Los Angeles, New York City, and to Hong Kong, where my brother was living. I stayed there for a year and a half, modeling for magazines and television. Living in Hong Kong, I did feel free—I didn't have to deal with my mother or father or their coldness. One day I got a phone call that my mother had been in a car accident. They called about a week after it happened, and it was a fairly life-threatening situation, she was rear-ended by a truck. But this was typical; my father informed me coolly, without emotion, after the fact.

Not even when she was on her deathbed did they allow emotions to show. Years later, my mother was scheduled to have surgery on a bad knee. Through the process of blood work, the doctors found uterine cancer. My dad called to tell me calmly that instead of simple knee surgery, my mom had her cancerous uterus removed and was in intensive care. I got off the phone, ready to just go about with my day, and a good friend said to me: "Well, aren't you going to go see her? It sounds like your mother is dying." I was divorced, with an eight-year-old daughter, so I put her in the car, and we drove from St. Louis to the hospital in Virginia and arrived late at night. It was very quiet in the hospital, and we were directed to the ICU. It was shocking to see my mother like this. She was swollen like a beached whale, three times larger than her normal self. My mother was conscious, but in very bad shape.

While having her uterus removed, her blood pressure dropped, and she was failing. My sister was very good with my mother, very nurturing and caring, and I wanted to be comforting to my mother as well. I walked into the room; my sister was on my mother's left side, and I walked around to my mother's right side. Her right hand started moving around, frantically. I thought she was reaching for me to hold my hand. But her fingers were moving with intensity, flailing around, and we noticed on the machines that her heart rate was really going up, reflecting how upset she was.

I took her hand but she kept fidgeting, and finally it became clear what she was doing: She was feeling my fingers, and ultimately she took my middle finger and stroked it and propped it up, in an aggressive way.

My mother had given me the finger. There was no denying this. My sister knew it too. By groping hard on my middle finger and sticking it up, she was saying to me, "F—k you." That was her final gesture and final words to me. My final words to my mother, who died soon after, were, "I love you, Mom."

When I got back to St. Louis, I thought hard about what she must have been so angry about. Maybe she felt I abandoned her, leaving her under the oppression of my father. But I just couldn't take responsibility for her sadness, the coldness, the lack of communication. This couldn't have been all about me. I was telling a friend about my mother giving me the finger on her deathbed, and he said to me: "Oh, well. She can't just leave it like that." I didn't understand what he meant, but two weeks after she passed away, I had one of those dreams too real to be a dream.

On her deathbed, she was inflated almost beyond recognition. In my dream, the swelling had gone down, and her body appeared healed. I was sitting and she was kneeling. The feeling toward my mother in the dream was as if she were my daughter who had misbehaved and needed my reassurance that I loved her. I was stroking her face and putting her hair behind her ear, consoling her, and letting her know everything was okay. I felt like there were words she needed to hear. So I got very close, touching her cheek, and whispered in her ear, "I love you." And she was looking up at me with the innocent and wide eyes of a child. Then suddenly, everything between us was okay.

That dream held so much resolution for me. Since that moment, really, I have felt like my mother is behind me. Whatever in our conscious lives was not spoken or done, in the cosmic life the true nature of my mother is inside of me. She seems more alive now than she ever was. She gives me the security I never had from her before. Through that dream, in which she became this completely innocent child who just needed reassurance, I was able to accept the true nature of her love. The love between a daughter and a mother is often too complicated to reveal in life. Now, the purity of my mother's love, the essence of her love, is the only thing that exists. Our relationship is no longer complicated; wherever I am now, and wherever my mother is, I always have the sense that she is covering my back. And it happened because symbolically, in that dream, I was able to love her as if she was my child, and she was asking for my forgiveness. As if by magic, this dream resolved all the torment and confusion over why she would give me the finger.

I think my mother's inner rebel motivates my inner rebel, as if they are linked by some kind of cosmic umbilical cord. Mom never knew about an annual exhibition I cofounded in St. Louis called Venus Envy, a collection of work by women artists, or my music videos, or much of anything else about me in the years before her death. She shut herself out of my life, probably because my artistic, divorced rebel side was too much of an affront to her suppressed rebel side. Now it feels as if she encourages my inner rebel, cheering me on in her afterlife as I do or say what she couldn't. We've become compadres, or would it be com-madres? The last words my mother heard from me were, "I love you." I meant it. Although she couldn't accept these things from me while she was living, she accepts them now and showers me with acceptance whenever I think of her.

I relate to Adrienne's feeling of omnipotent love as my mom lies sweet and pure and weak. As she is going, I am coming into my own, boosted by her zeal and resilience. You can actually feel the infusion of a waning mother's spirit. Adrienne calls the connection a "cosmic umbilical cord," a transference of maternal energy that is amplified after death.

On a trip back to Chicago, I run into one of my dear friends from childhood, Patricia Hefner, who grew up in our neighborhood as one of twelve children. I had not seen Patricia for thirty-two years, and we talked about our kids and our mothers and the old days playing Mancala and climbing trees at the playground. I knew her mom very well, and she knew mine. Speaking about the demands of raising only one child, Patricia, fifty-two, a retired administrator from the county court system, marveled how her mother managed to juggle the needs of a virtual tribe that also included Mary, Danny, David, Georgia, Terry, Michael, Jean, Paul, Virginia, Jill, and John. The Hefner dozen went on to produce forty-four children of their own. Five years after her mother's death from lung disease, Patricia told me how her mother and their grandmother continue to serve as the backbone of their lives. Indeed, it was because of her mother that Patricia had the strength to hold her head high at the age of twenty-three and have a child out of wedlock, a daughter, Allison, who recently graduated with a master's degree in clinical psychology.

My mother was one of eleven children, so she knew how to deal with crowds. You just didn't get away with complaining about anything. If we said, "So and so was mean to me," she'd always say, "Save your breath. Consider the source," which meant: You are way better than she is, so don't bother with her. I still think of her words and am able to cruise through most obstacles that come my way.

We grew up in a three-bedroom house, with only one full bathroom, and my father worked three jobs, one as a mail carrier. My mom worked nights at the Federal Reserve Bank, from 11 P.M. to 7 A.M. So, we kind of raised each other, but my mom definitely set the structure and the rules. Each person was assigned to a group that did chores together; the four oldest were together, the four middle, and the four babies.

As soon as we were old enough to work, we all were expected to take jobs after school. I worked at Jack in the Box. And we did whatever my mom needed done with the younger kids. I only realized recently, after she died a few years ago, just what a huge responsibility she had and how well she did it. How did she do it? With twelve children, all of us were always dressed and prepared for school dances, proms, and plays, and our homework got done. She made a big dinner every night, and we generally sat down together; usually it was potatoes, chicken, and corn. We never had a lot of money, but she somehow got it together for all of us. And regrettably, now that she's gone, I wish I had asked her just how she did what she did. It was really an incredible, even superhuman, feat.

She didn't keep a flow chart with chores; you just knew to pitch in and do whatever needed to be done. Yet, somehow my mom managed to give each child what he or she needed.

I can't say I ever really felt neglected. But I'm not floating down the river of the Nile in some la-la fantasy. There were things that went on in my family, and people just sort of looked the other way. Instead of coming home after work, dad would go to the bars. My mom accepted it, and she dealt with it the best that she could. I will say this to my father's credit: He did not drink in the house; my mother felt that alcohol did not belong around children. So even for holiday parties there was no alcohol.

Those nights that he'd be out with his friends, we'd be sitting on the front porch with my mom. I remember those hot summer Chicago nights, and my mom would be telling us story after story, and we'd be huddled around her. And then when the grandchildren came, we'd still be huddled around her on that porch.

When I was fourteen years old, this tall boy moved in down the street. He was a year behind me in school, his mother was a widow, and we became friends, with some mild flirting always going on. When he was home from college in the summer of 1976 we took some classes together. I was twenty-three at the time. Then he came home for the following summer, and we started dating. I got pregnant by him in October of 1977. I would call our relationship borderline-serious, and it would have probably gotten more serious had I not gotten pregnant.

He absolutely did not want a child; his argument was to put a dollar value on the child: "We don't have money to have a child. We can't do it. I can't do it." And money was never an issue for me. Growing up how I did, I knew that money always showed up whenever you needed it. When I heard him say that I thought, "Buddy, you have no idea what it takes to raise children, and it's not about money." Basically, he freaked out. I told him that I was still having the baby; in my Catholic family, and in my heart, I can tell you abortion was not an option. If I terminated the pregnancy, I could never live with myself. That baby would be always looking at me.

Well, he didn't like my decision. And basically, his attitude was, "This is your problem." I found out I was pregnant in the middle of November and did not tell my mother right away, even though I was living at home. Then it was Thanksgiving and then it was Christmas, and I kept thinking, "I can't tell my mom on the holidays." But I started showing. I had been very thin, and then, well, I wasn't so thin.

Some of my sisters noticed that something must be up because I started to look different, and I'm sure I was acting different. Finally, I admitted my situation to my mom when I was driving her downtown to her job. She told me she had been to the family doctor with my younger brother. My family doctor knew what was going on with me. And I said, "Oh, really, did he say anything about me?" She said, "Why, what's wrong with you?" And I remember this like it was yesterday: I said, "Nothing's wrong, mom. I'm having a baby in July." She said, "What do you want to do?" I said, "I don't want to get married." And she goes, "Good, then don't." She asked me if my boyfriend knew, and I said yes, but that he wasn't a part of this. Then she said something that was just so like her: "Well, that's fine. It will be nice to have the pitter-patter of little feet in the house again."

And Allison and I lived in my mother's house until she was four years old. The father of this child didn't give me the support that I needed, but my family and friends were there for me. He has only seen our daughter once: at the blood test that I had done to prove paternity. Once I had this child, my interests were not on getting married; they were on Allison. She was my priority, and although it would have been nice to meet someone that could be a father in her life, that just didn't happen. You know, I have been on my own really my whole life, and it's OK with me. Allison has turned out to be a wonderful, smart young lady who is very independent and very confident.

I credit my mother with giving us the tools to know how to get things done in life. Because she welcomed us into her house, Allison and I always had a strong foundation, even if I didn't have a husband, and she didn't have a father. I'm a very strong woman, and my daughter is very strong too, and that's my mother in us. Thank God for my mother. The day I found out I was pregnant, November 14, 1977, I knew I was going to have this child and raise this child, come hell or high water. Money or no money. Husband or no husband. I knew I could always get a job. I knew I had family that would always help me. Watching my mother raise twelve good children, I knew I could do anything. She made me feel like everything was going to be OK, and it was OK, it was more than OK.

And as far as Allison goes, I really felt I did a great job. She is absolutely a gift, and I've known that from the minute I found out I was pregnant. That day I discovered I was pregnant, I said: "This is fine. I can do this." I watched my mother roll up her sleeves and do just about anything. Of course, I knew I could do anything too. I was raised knowing that if you see something in front of you that needs to be picked up, you just pick it up; you don't walk around it. You deal with life; you don't complain about it.

And I would say even if there were twelve of us, we each felt unique. My mother made each of her children feel like he or she was the best, most important person in her life. When she died, all of us were at the wake, and it was funny—we were all saying, "She liked me better than she liked any of you." Even the dozens of grandchildren were saying that to each other. "Grandma liked me best." My mom had a way of making each child and each grandchild feel as if he or she were her one and only.

She was unquestionably the pillar of our family, and the pillar of my life. But she wasn't the kind of pillar that made it so when she left, you'd fall apart. She was the kind of pillar that lasts eternally. Like I said, she taught this daughter how to carry on with her life, no matter what happens, and to be thankful for what you have and not depressed over what you don't have. When my mom died, everyone was saying to my dad what wonderful children he has. And he told each one of them, "Don't thank me. Thank Mary. It was all because of my wife."

A mother, even in her absence, "is the power inside you," writes Sue Monk Kidd in her novel *The Secret Life of Bees*, and that power is eternal. As I face the loss of my mother, I am seduced by the notion that we can birth a new self and mother that person through our own internal reserves and spiritual exploration.

I seek out Reverend Katherine Klemstine, the chaplain of my local hospice, Hospice of the Chesapeake, to learn more about the eternal mother-daughter dance, and how the divine enters into the healing process. She speaks not only from work experience with the dying but also from her own soulful transaction at the time of her mother's death.

Klemstine, a small woman with high cheekbones and silvery hair, helps families with the heavy emotional lifting of coping with terminally ill loved ones. Like Elisabeth Kubler-Ross, Klemstine's decades at the bedsides of the dying have convinced her that this life is not all there is. Raised as a Catholic, she is particularly fascinated by the concept of the Divine Feminine, the nurturing, holy feminine spirit personified by Sophia, known in the Jewish scriptures as humankind's co-creator with God. Sophia is the feminine face of the masculine God who entices us in the book of Proverbs: "Come to me, my children, that I may bless your ways . . . Whoever find me, finds love and shall dwell forevermore with Love and Wisdom." Klemstine also points to Mother Earth as a nurturing universal female archetype who can comfort those in need just as a mother comforts a child.

When I interviewed evangelist Billy Graham for UPI, he had incandescent eyes and a light to his face that seemed to me inhuman and holy. Klemstine's aura is like that, too. She positively glows, and when she looks at me, it is as if she is looking right through me. Here are some of her observations, from her sacred perch on the cusp of two worlds:

As a result of what I witness in my work, I believe when a mother is dying there is a meshing of the mother's and daughter's souls. A daughter has had a primal connection to her mother her entire life, and when her mother's soul leaves the earth, the two women still remain profoundly linked. The awareness of such a bond can free you as well. It's almost as though you have an agreement with your mother to walk through this life together, and when she passes, there is a metamorphosis in your own self and soul. In my mother's death, she released me into becoming my true, healed self.

My sister Teresa and I were at my mother's bedside when she was passing away. We held her for a few minutes, and she said, "Do you think it's time for me to go? Do you think God wants me now?" And my sister, who is a nurse said, "Mom, are you ready for God to take you?" And between gasping breaths she said, "Yes, I am." So then I said a brief prayer, "Dear God, please take your beautiful daughter Frances in your loving light and hold her in your loving arms." Then my mother's gaze shifted, she breathed one more time, and she passed away in our arms. Her head was resting in my hands, and I felt her soul slip right through my fingers. I feel that's a gift that my mother gave me. She allowed me to be part of a sacred intimacy that we'd never had before. We were one.

It can be a blessing to be at the bedside of your dying mother in those moments you have, talking quietly or sitting silently. I've seen daughters taking care of mothers who had been abusive to them during their childhood. Yet the daughter was there, providing end-of-life care for her mother, and I've seen the peace that comes over both of them. I've seen other daughters who have had difficult relationships with their mothers speaking of their thankfulness for something small yet profound in an entire life that they will always remember. It may have only been a few perfect moments in a long imperfect relationship that affect how the daughter is able to go forward in her life. Yet, mystical healing still can take place.

My closest times with my mother growing up were when we were sitting in the backyard on summer evenings, looking out across the farmlands, watching the sunset and the clouds. I still feel her most when I sit and watch the sun set. The absolute power of the mother-daughter genetic connection is undeniable. I felt very clearly with my mother's passing that I am my mother. How can I not be? I came from her womb. So much of me is who she is. And because of my faith, I do believe in the next life and that spiritually we remain together. Although the physical loss is as if something has been torn away at the level of the soul.

I often hear daughters who have lost their mothers speak of an overwhelming awareness of the power of that relationship. Women are shocked at how profound the feeling is, looking back at just what a mother meant to them throughout a lifetime, which may be realized only after they have passed. Because of the power of this bond, I encourage women to always attempt to heal unresolved anger, even if their dying mothers are not conscious or able to communicate. She may not be able to respond, but a mother is aware, and listening, in her heart.

And I hear daughters' words come out with tears and love, and not anger. In those last moments, no matter how old the daughter is, they are speaking as a child to a mother, telling them things in a very loving and gentle way, acknowledging the need for some kind of forgiveness or acceptance. It is important to speak your heart, to meet your mother truthfully in the last moments, to acknowledge that perhaps she wasn't always there for you, but yet to say this: "You're my mother. And I love you."

When my dying patients speak of someone who is waiting to greet them on the other side, often it is a mother who is reaching out with a comforting hand. Our mothers bring us into this world, and they help us out of this world. I hear elderly women crying out like children to their mothers. And when our mothers die to go to their mothers, we then continue to heal their ancestral unfinished work. You can go out and develop yourself, but you can't escape your mother.

A dying mother has much to teach a daughter, and it's all about love. From our mothers we learn how to love and we learn how to receive love. And by learning love from our mothers, we learn how to love in relationships, how to love ourselves, and it's also the way we learn how to love God. So a mother's love is an introduction into the very nature of love itself.

I am not a hospice chaplain privy to the last words of countless mothers. What I do know from more than a hundred interviews is that mothers continue to speak to their daughters, whether they reside in our world or in the next.

Simone is a commercial photographer's assistant who used to speak to her mother, Kate, three times a day. They lived in neighboring suburbs and saw one another twice a week. Five years ago, Kate was on her morning walk shortly after 7:30 A.M. when a school bus sped around the corner on her serene street and literally plowed her down. She was sixty-nine and in perfect health.

Simone's daughter Maddie was four when her grand-mother died, and she refuses to accept the notion that death means someone is forever gone. To this day, about once or twice a month, Maddie demands of her mother, "I want to talk to Grandma." And Simone, fifty-one, makes it happen.

The first time Maddie asked me to talk to Grandma, I just said, "OK, she's here, honey." And Maddie asked: "Did you see me swim today, Grandma? I went into the deep end for the first time." And I don't know what came over me, but it felt like it wasn't me controlling the words that came out. My voice changed, it got deeper like my mother's, and I answered my daughter as if I were my mother. "Yes Maddie, I can't believe what a big girl you are. I saw you swim in your pretty red swimsuit, and you were so brave."

So we do this a lot now. Maddie is now ten, but she still says to me, usually when I'm lying next to her, putting her to bed, "Can I talk to Grandma?" And she talks to my mother through me, tells her about a birthday party she went to or a soccer game she played in. And I answer as if I were Grandma, and the words just come pouring out; I don't have to think at all. It's strange because in a way, I am Mommy and Grandma now. When I answer my daughter, it's my mother's heart talking.

I realize that a story of a dead mother coming alive to speak to her granddaughter may raise some eyebrows. But from the stories poured into my tape recorder, I believe that anything is possible when it comes to our mothers, and nothing is surprising. They are omnipotent creatures. Adrienne's mother came back to her in a dream and totally revitalized their relationship. Here is another story that demonstrates the supernatural force between mother and daughter, in life and in death.

Lee's Story 🌿

Lee is a television producer who recently celebrated her forty-first birthday. Adopted as an infant, Lee felt an urgent compulsion to find her birth mother when she hit thirty. As she puts it: "I didn't look like anybody else. I didn't feel like anything else. I needed to find that connection." Relentless sleuthing led her to a blood relative, the brother of her birth mother, who shared some astounding news: Her biological mom was a onetime beauty queen named Betty who once dated Joe DiMaggio. Pregnant, unmarried, and plagued with mental illness, Betty landed in a hospital where she was given shock treatments. Her baby, whom she named April Lee, was quickly put up for adoption. Lee's uncle said that Betty was now a street person in New York City, on the Upper West Side. And he turned over some family pictures.

Lee went to New York, blanketed that neighborhood with flyers, and through a series of phone calls and contacts managed to find the still-flamboyant Betty in a homeless shelter on 107th Street. Wiping tears from her eyes, Lee describes the day she found her mother: "Meeting Betty has filled a hunger I've been carrying around my whole life. It was a completion I had never known."

Lee's story is about a daughter's brief elation and instant connection with a woman she had been separated from for twenty-five years.

I'd been searching for about six weeks to find Betty. The only information I had was that she was last seen at the intersection of 77th and Broadway over by a park that at the time was called Needle Park; it's no longer there. I had several copies of her photograph made, and I put information on the back that said, "Do you know this woman? If you do, please contact me," along with my phone numbers. Most people did know her. She seemed to be a fixture in that neighborhood. And everyone seemed to like her. She was a big personality. They would talk about how she would sing on the street.

I had a strange feeling that day; I surrendered to a higher power, thinking: "Look, I'm not in charge here. If I'm supposed to find her, I'll find her. But if I don't, I'll accept that." But I did have this overwhelming feeling that she was alive and out there for me to find that day. It also happened to be Friday the 13th and Good Friday. I ended up in a church where I talked to a man named Father O'Connor. He gave me a list of places to look where he thought she might hang out. Last on the list was a place called Project Reachout, which supported homeless people all over New York City. I walked in and held up the picture to the receptionist and she said, "That's Betty." And I said, "Have you seen her lately? Is she OK?" And she said, "Oh, yeah, I've seen her. She's one of our clients." And everything felt like it was buzzing around me. I said, "Well, I'm her daughter." She told me to wait while she got the director, who would have to talk to me before I could see Betty.

All of a sudden, while I was sitting in the waiting room, in walks Betty. And she walks right past me, and I knew immediately that it was her; there was no mistaking. And she turned and looked at me and nodded and smiled, then went over to the coffee machine and poured herself a cup of coffee. I was thinking, "Oh my God, that is my mother. And she has no idea it's me." Just then the director walks in, I tell her my story, and then I say, "I want to meet Betty. She's my mother."

Well, the director and other staff were kind of dumbfounded; they didn't quite know what to do. They said they had never had anybody come in and claim someone before. Then the director said to me, "OK, here's what we're going to do. You go have lunch. We'll talk to Betty. If she remembers having you, we will introduce you. But if she doesn't, we can't." That was the longest hour of my life. I was a wreck. I couldn't eat anything.

They had her social worker speak to her, and they asked if she remembered having a baby at Crownsville, which is a mental hospital outside of Baltimore. And she did remember having me. So that was a huge relief. I was brought into this room, and they went to go get Betty. The director, Madeline, brought Betty in and said, "I'd like to introduce you to your visitor today. She's come a long way to see you, and she's been very worried about how you are doing." And without missing one beat, a completely charming Betty said, "Hi, honey. How ya doing?" She was just loaded with enthusiasm and had this incredibly warm smile. I was still in a state of shock, but I was trying to make sure every cell of my being was soaking up every single nuance I could smell and see and feel in this moment. And then I realize I'm looking at me, in many ways. From the smoky blue eyes, dark around the edges, to the hand movements to the facial expressions, our mannerisms were almost completely the same. Same humor. It was like being part of somebody else for the first time in my life. Then

Madeline said, "I'd like to introduce you to your daughter. This is Lee." I searched Betty's eyes for some glimmer of recognition or acceptance. I felt as if I couldn't breathe. This was the moment I'd been waiting for my whole life."

Betty looked straight into my eyes real hard, like she was looking for some sort of an answer or something familiar. Then, you could almost see it click when she had the realization: "Oh my God, this is her." She started crying, and I just kind of made a joke and said, "You know, you sure are a hard person to find." Then she said quietly, "I sure am glad you found me so I don't have to worry about you anymore." She reached over and took my hand, her hand was bigger than mine, and her nails were done, so she still had some hints of the old glamour queen Betty.

I went over and hugged her. I didn't cry. I was sort of having an out-of-body experience. What was most overwhelming was the fact that I felt such a strong connection with this woman without having shared any of my life with her. I felt like I was home, probably for the first time in my life. I showed her some of her old pictures I had dug up, when she was a very beautiful showgirl, and she got very excited and started to show them to everybody saying, "Look that's me, back when I had my teeth."

We ended up getting in a van to drive up to the building where Project Reachout provided apartments for homeless people. She wanted to show me where she lived. She lit up a Salem, and she was puffing away all the way up to the apartment. When we got there, she paraded me around the lobby, telling everyone: "This is my daughter. Her name is April Lee. She came and found me today." Later we talked, and she told me that when I was born, she was considered mentally ill and told to give her baby up for adoption. She said, "They let me hold you once and then they took you away. I never knew what happened to you."

I said to her: "Betty, your birthday is in a month. I promise I'll come back. We'll do something fun." The whole car ride back to Baltimore, I kept saying, "Holy shit. Did this really happen?" It was so emotionally earth shattering. Basically, the entire foundation of my life was just re-done in a matter of one day.

That feeling I got from the moment I met Betty, of being home, comfortably familiar, connected—I never had that, ever, ever, ever. I never looked like anybody else. I could never look at someone with a knowing nod and feel we're thinking the same thing. This was a turning point in my life. I know lots of adopted children don't choose to do this, but for me, I was really searching to find my mother. And I found her, and through that, I found myself. I don't know what I was expecting or looking for when I started searching for Betty. I just knew it was something I never had before. I just knew there was something else out there that would make me feel different and better.

My adoptive mother tried really hard to do all the right things. And I had a privileged childhood. I had piano lessons and horseback riding lessons and went to Europe three times. I went to private schools. But my mom and I were just very different. She never got who I was. She was very tight and controlling. I'm a more free-spirited person. And there was never a yielding to the other in either of us. I knew my mom loved me, and I loved my mom. But there was a whole aspect of myself that felt very alone. I always felt that nobody understood who I was, and I just had this incredible yearning to find that person who could appreciate me, unconditionally, and not try to change me. From the ages of eleven to eighteen, I basically shut myself down to my adoptive mother and never let her in.

Then, I meet Betty. And she just gets me immediately. I am deeply connected to someone, finally, in a spiritual way that words cannot even describe. I had been calling Project Reachout every morning, talking to Betty and Madeline about plans for my visit. I was so excited to see her again. Then, one morning, I get a phone call from Madeline. She said, "Betty died in her sleep." My head was exploding. I felt rage all through my body. I just found my birth mother; how could this happen? Why would I live a whole life, find her, then lose her after one day together?

But I did get the chance to feel and touch and breathe her. Meeting Betty, only for a couple of hours, gave me a feeling I've never had with anyone else. There was just something almost unspoken, this connection between a mother and a daughter. It transcends so many things. I never knew what it was until I had it, even though I had it for a very short time. Here it is, years later, and I still feel connected and grounded. I will never forget that moment that Betty looked into my eyes, and I just knew deep down that somebody loved me totally. At her funeral, the church was filled with disheveled homeless people who loved Betty. And I felt proud to be her daughter, thankful for our one day together. It was the first step to answer all of the questions that had haunted me: Who am I? Do my freckles mean I'm Irish? Turns out they did. I studied Betty's face so hard and absorbed every wrinkle, every crease. I was starving for familiarity.

Meeting Betty was a validation of who I am and that it's okay to be this way. Because suddenly there's someone look-

ing back at you that's a reflection in the mirror. When I
looked in her eyes, there was a sense of mischievous joy that
I've always felt. It was almost like a jolt of electricity for me.
No one ever looked at me that way before. She knew what I
knew, without saying a word. I think that if I hadn't had that
intervention in my life, I would have crashed and burned a
long time ago. In many ways, it was mystical and magical.
When she touched me, I was sailing.

Long after I leave Lee, her words "I was home" stay with me. Lee spent only a fraction of one day with her birth mother, yet she immediately knew her deeply, and hungered to know more. I've had fifty years with Helene Krasnow, and it's still not enough.

Months after meeting Lee, her odyssey propels me on a journey to walk the streets my mother walked, in her youth and in her early years as a young mother. I wanted to do this while she was alive, so we could talk about what I see and feel and wonder about. First stop, Paris, where I am overcome with absolute knowing that I am my mother's daughter. I wind through the brick-paved streets on the Left Bank of the Seine, where Helene Steinberg grew from girl to woman, drinking deeply of French café culture, under the gaze of ancient gargoyles. As I travel in 2005 where she traveled in the 1940s, there is little that is foreign about the people or the buildings thousands of miles from my home in Annapolis. Here, too, I am home, embedded in my mother's past and the path that led to the creation of me, and of my own passions and path.

The sky in late February is as gray as the stone walls of Notre Dame, making the flower boxes pop out as if they were fluorescent. Pleasure and gloom, the contrasts in my heart, mirror the black and white shades of my mom, a woman who was either very up or very down, rarely settled on a plateau. I am assaulted by pastel silk scarves wrapped around French women with attitude, by storefront shelves laden with ripe cheeses and smoked meats, by sullen passersby, smoking and sighing. My mother shoots through me in one blast of wind off the Seine.

I tell her about my trip to France one afternoon at her kitchen table in Chicago. On some days of her illness, my mother is very chatty; this is not one of them. Yet she is clamorous in her expressions. Her eyes dart and flash, and she laughs when I recall my visit with her cousins Marcel and Ferdinand and Gigi over bottles of Bordeaux, in a restaurant my mother used to go to long ago. As I am talking, I am feeding her bits of gooey Saint André cheese on French bread, and with each bite she takes, I feel the soft wetness inside her mouth. It reminds me of when I fed my babies their first solid food. The circle of life, death, and birth is heavy on me, and I feel compelled to see the place I was raised, alongside the woman who raised me. After our snack, we take an afternoon drive out to Oak Park, a twenty-five-minute car ride away.

We park in front of 926 Forest Avenue, and I am remembering what it was like growing up in a house of Slavic-French customs in a village of freckled, old-line Americans. I was ashamed to bring friends home to my mother, who sounded like Zsa Zsa Gabor and didn't belong to a tennis club as their moms did. Our kitchen reeked of Roquefort left out on the counter, or liver and other organs sautéing stovetop in onions and oil. I am staring at my house and smell a pungent potpourri of every food my mother has served me. The green shutters are now painted brown, but other than that, our house appears nearly unchanged. My mother points with a shaking finger out the car window and says in a barely audible whisper, "My cherry tree." We are both recalling that tree, resplendent in our backyard with pink blossoms, and its sour fruit that the squirrels liked better than we did.

My childhood bedroom faces the street, and I picture my rattan furniture and peace-sign poster still in there. I am fourteen again, lying on my orange bedspread, listening to Carly Simon and talking on my blue princess dial phone. This bedroom is where I fled to cry over bad boyfriends or the demands of my mother. She is remembering everything too; I see it in her face. We drive down the alley that leads to our back garage where she parked her white Chrysler with its pointy taillights. We sit in silence as we both look at the playground next door that was turned into an ice skating rink every winter. My sister and brother and I would race across the alley every day after school, skates flung over our shoulders, dash home for a quick dinner, and then go back and skate under the lights.

My mother tells me something I never knew. "When you were in school I used to skate by myself." That is a wondrous vision, my mom in her thirties and forties, red-cheeked and floating on the ice, agile and fit and alone. She seems to be imagining her white figure skates while she sits next to her little girl, who is now a half-century old.

We get back to her apartment and drink some Cabernet. My plane leaves in two hours. We are both tired from our outing, and we're not talking. I am thinking what she is thinking: When will we see each other again? I am sad and I am happy. What an honor to be with my mother at the end of a life that was long and complete, and not cut short by early disease or an accident. When there is no more anger, it's amazing how much space opens up for compassion.

My mother's caregiver, Donna, drives the three of us to Midway Airport, and I boast about my children, about Zane's mastery of Mozart on the piano and his twin Jack's emerging talents as a magician. I tell her that Theo is about to get his driver's permit and that Isaac, at the age of thirteen, is reading *The Seven Habits of Highly Successful People*. I assure her that her grandchildren are smart and beautiful, "just like you are, Mom," knowing she may never see them again.

"Kiss the kids," she says. "And give me a kiss." I grab my black canvas bag and come around to the passenger side of the car. As I kiss her on both cheeks and on the forehead, I hear her humming "Dites moi pourquoi la vie est belle," the French song that means "Tell me why life is beautiful," which she used to sing to her three toddlers when she had us together in one bathtub. She interrupts herself with a firm, "I love you, Iya," then continues humming, her mind drifting back to Forest Avenue and to my father and to France. As I'm just about to enter the terminal, I quickly turn around for one last look at my mother in her silver Volvo. She is waving, a slow Miss America wave, and her eyes are staring straight ahead.

Bibliography ✍

Aspects of the Feminine
C. G. Jung
Routledge (2004)

Basic Freud: Psychoanalytic Thought for the 21st Century
Michael Kahn
Basic Books (2002)

The Bonesetter's Daughter
Amy Tan
Putnam Adult (2001)

*The Essence of Buddhism: How to Bring
Spiritual Meaning into Every Day*
Carole M. Cusack
Barnes and Noble (2001)

*Female Authority: Empowering Women Through
Psychotherapy*
Polly Young-Eisendrath and Florence L. Wiedemann
Guilford Press; reprint edition (1990)

Fruitful: A Real Mother in the Modern World
Anne Richardson Roiphe
Houghton Mifflin (1996)

The Great Mother
Erich Neumann; translated by Ralph Manheim
Bollingen; reprint, 2nd edition (1972)

A Little Book on Love
Jacob Needleman
Currency (1996)

Little Women
Louisa May Alcott
First published in 1869
Sterling (2004)

Lovingkindness: The Revolutionary Art of Happiness
Sharon Salzberg and Jon Kabat-Zinn
Shambhala (2004)

Magic Orange Tree and Other Haitian Folktales
Diane Wolkstein
Schocken (1997)

Marjorie Morningstar
Herman Wouk
First published in 1955
Back Bay Books (1992)

Mommie Dearest
Christina Crawford
William Morrow (1978)

Mother-Daughter Wisdom: Creating a Legacy of Physical and Emotional Health
Christiane Northrup, M.D.
Bantam (2005)

Mother Love
Candace Flynt
Farrar, Straus and Giroux (1987)

My Life So Far
Jane Fonda
Random House (2005)

My Mother/My Self
Nancy Friday
Delacorte Press (1977)

O'Keeffe and Stieglitz: An American Romance
Benita Eisler
Penguin (1992)

On Death and Dying
Elisabeth Kubler-Ross
Scribner; reprint edition (1997)

Principles of General Psychology
Gregory A. Kimble
John Wiley & Sons, 5th edition (1980)

The Second Sex
Simone de Beauvoir
First published in 1949
Random House (1974)

The Secret Life of Bees
Sue Monk Kidd
Viking Adult; Good Morning America edition (2002)

Successful Aging
John Rowe, M.D., and Robert Kahn, Ph.D.
Pantheon (1998)

Surrendering to Marriage: Husbands, Wives, and Other Imperfections
Iris Krasnow
Miramax Books (2001)

Surrendering to Yourself: You Are Your Own Soul Mate
Iris Krasnow
Miramax Books (2003)

A Very Easy Death
Simone de Beauvoir
First published in 1964
Warner Books (1977)

Acknowledgments ❦

Every woman in my close circle of colleagues and friends had a hand in the creation of this book. It was as if this work were a huge, steaming pot of stew, and we were all standing around it in my kitchen, pouring in little dollops from our hearts. Because of their generosity of spirit, *I Am My Mother's Daughter* is a composite piece that embraces all our mothers and the universal experience of being an adult daughter.

First, an enormous thank you to Jo Ann Miller, Editorial Director of Basic Books, who believed in this project within minutes of hearing about it. Wise and patient, Jo Ann coached and challenged me, shaping my prose with her compassion and humor. I am also deeply grateful to Kara Baskin, a young woman of great intellect and gustiness who serves as the development editor in the office of my literary agent, Gail Ross. Kara pushed me to be brave and clear, with relentless questioning of every phrase. Erica Naone, a recent graduate of St. John's College, helped me pore through piles of literature on mothers and daughters and aging. With her keen eye and love of language, Erica was startling in her ability to uncover obscure anecdotes and quotes.

I could not have turned my dozens of interviews into a cohesive document without Laura Hollon, my longtime technological assistant who is masterful at smoothing out every computer glitch.

And to my agent, Gail Ross, you are the smartest and the best. Gail insisted from the start that I—a mother of four sons—should write about mothers and daughters. I resisted, telling Gail: "But I don't have girls." Her response was this: "But you have a mother, and so does—or did—every other woman in the world. Women love to dish about their moms." Gail was right, and dish they did. I can't thank all of my chatty and honest sources enough, the 116 brave daughters who spoke to me for this book through lots of tears and laughter. Although some of you aren't named, please know that your voices and passion permeate each page. It was a difficult labor to get to this joyous birth, a gestation that coincided with the demise of my own 85-year-old mom, who nearly died a dozen times during these months of writing.

I could not have composed *I Am My Mother's Daughter* without the solace and strength of longtime girlfriends who never failed to show up with a bottle of wine or bolstering words at precisely the right moment. I am eternally appreciative to Randi Altschuler, Debbie Butler, Marcy Curland, Susan Dalsimer, Ellyn Dooley, Sarah Greene, Moe Hanson, Simone Lecat, Fran Marshall, Jan Miller, Terry Rubin, Amy Rudnick, Gail Watkins, and the Ladies of the Book Club.

To Chuck Anthony, my steadfast husband, and our sons, Theo, Isaac, Zane, and Jack; you five loyal and loving men ground me, excite me, and fill me with the courage and conviction to write the truth about family relationships. Finally, I'd like to thank my sister, Frances, and brother, Greg, who will be by my side as we cope with our transforming lives when our mom is no longer here. It is because of Frances, who manages my mother's health care, that we've been blessed to have Helene Krasnow this long.